PLAYS of THE WILD WEST

Grades K–3

Published by Smith and Kraus, Inc.
PO Box 127, Lyme, NH 03768

Manufactured in the United States of America
First Edition: May 1997
10 9 8 7 6 5 4 3 2 1
Cover and Text Design by Julia Hill/Freedom Hill Design
Cover Illustration by Aline Ordman

The Library of Congress Cataloging-In-Publication Data
McCullough, L.E.

Plays of the Wild West: grades K–3 / L.E. McCullough. —1st ed.
p. cm. — (Young actors series)
Includes bibliographical references.

Summary: A collection of twelve original plays dramatizing songs, folklore, historical events, and larger-than-life characters of the Wild West.

ISBN 1-57525-104-3
1. Frontier and pioneer life—West (U.S.) —Juvenile drama.
2. Children's plays, American. [1. Frontier and pioneer life—West (U.S.) —Drama. 2. West (U.S.) —Drama. 3. Plays.]
I. Title. II. Series: Young Actors Series.

PS3563.C35297P59   1997
812'.54—dc21   97-14729
                    CIP
                AC

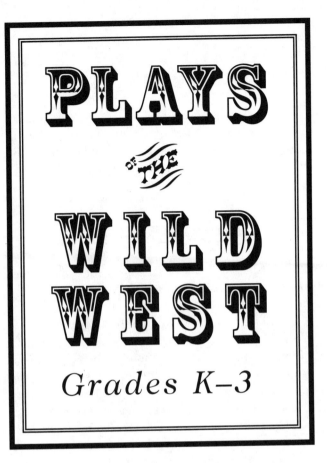

PLAYS OF THE WILD WEST

Grades K–3

L.E. McCullough

YOUNG ACTORS SERIES

SK

A Smith and Kraus book

DEDICATION

To all our courageous ancestors—native peoples and settlers—who took part in one of the most tumultuous periods in human history, the Wild West. May we cherish and preserve the nation they created and the bountiful land they left us.

ACKNOWLEDGMENTS

The author wishes to thank the following for professional literary development and career support:

J.D. Nelson of Deadwood, South Dakota, a consummate actor and real-life cowboy; Joe Englander of Austin, Texas, whose photographs capture the ancient spirit of the modern West; Professor Dwayne Thorpe of Washington & Jefferson University, from whom I first heard many classic Western songs of his Kansas boyhood including *Zebra Dun*; folklorist W.K. McNeil, Ph.D. of the Ozark Folk Center, Mountain View, Arkansas; Lincoln Maazel of Pittsburgh; Jim Williams of Albuquerque, New Mexico; Linda Warder and her 5th-Grade Drama Club of Orchard Park Elementary School, Carmel, Indiana; Jana Foster of the Spanish Department, Indiana University–Purdue University at Indianapolis; my parents, who instilled my lifelong love of history with a Davy Crockett coonskin cap and Flint McCullough Wagon Train holster—*and*—my wife, Jane McCullough, a genuine Wild West pepperpot if there ever was one.

CONTENTS

THE AUTHOR

L.E. McCULLOUGH, PH.D. is a playwright, composer and ethnomusicologist whose studies in music and folklore have spanned cultures throughout the world. Formerly Assistant Director of the Indiana University School of Music at Indianapolis and a touring artist with Young Audiences, Inc., Dr. McCullough is the Administrative Director of the Humanities Theatre Group at Indiana University-Purdue University at Indianapolis. Winner of the 1995 Playwrights' Preview Productions Emerging Playwright Award for his stage play *Blues for Miss Buttercup*, he is the author of *The Complete Irish Tinwhistle Tutor*, *Favorite Irish Session Tunes* and *St. Patrick Was a Cajun*, three highly acclaimed music instruction books, and has performed on the soundtracks for the PBS specials *The West* and *Lewis and Clark*. Since 1991, Dr. McCullough has received 35 awards in 26 national literary competitions and has had 178 poem and short story publications in 90 North American literary journals. He is a member of The Dramatists Guild, Inc. and the American Conference for Irish Studies.

FOREWORD

Backward, turn backward, oh time with your wheels,
Airplanes and wagons and automobiles;
Give me once more my sombrero and flaps,
Spurs, flannel shirt, slicker and chaps.
Put a six-shooter or two in my hand,
Show me a yearling to rope and to brand,
Out where the sagebrush is dusty and gray
Make me a cowboy again for a day.

"Cowboy Again for a Day," Western folk song

The twelve plays in this book celebrate an epic period in American history—the transformation of the Western frontier from an unmapped wilderness inhabited by a few hundred thousand native tribespeople at the start of the 19th century into a fenced-off, dammed-up, staked-out region teeming with farms, factories, lumber mills, oil rigs, railroads, ranches and cities supporting millions of newcomers from around the world at the start of 20th. They cover a wide spectrum of historic events, ranging from the Lewis & Clark Expedition and Texas cattle drives to the Alaska Gold Rush and the settling of early San Francisco. Most importantly for educators, *Plays of the Wild West* presents not only well-known Western icons such as Annie Oakley, Sitting Bull, Buffalo Bill Cody and the Pony Express; it provides concise glimpses of the folks who did the real work of taming the frontier: homesteaders, railroaders, miners, missionaries, working cowboys and the West's first settlers, the Native Americans.

The story of the American West is, in fact, a diffuse rainbow of many remarkable stories celebrating the many remarkable people who left the familiar Old World for a New World of unceasing danger and unlimited promise. My ancestors first arrived on the North American continent from Wales in 1630 and settled in rural New England, each successive generation edging farther west until 1846 when they reached Wisconsin and Iowa, then the western boundary of the "civilized" United States. In 1865-66, my great-grandfather George McCollough served as a 19-year-old army corporal at Ft. Rice in Dakota Territory ("on the Indian Frontier," noted his obituary), and then returned home to St. Ansgar, Iowa, and an uneventful life as a teacher and commercial traveler. That was as far west as any of my family ventured until I taught at a folk music camp in Humboldt County, California, in the mid-1980s. Not much of a rousing pioneer pedigree, admittedly, yet I distinctly remember that the first toy I begged my parents to buy me as a child was a six-gun cap pistol like Hopalong Cassidy and The Lone Ranger carried. Even for modern Americans living far from the coyote's howl, the West exerts a continuing fascination.

The *Plays of the Wild West* series has been designed to combine with studies in other disciplines: history, costume, language, dance, music, social studies, etc. If you are a music teacher and want to add some more period songs and music to any of the plays, go ahead and make it a class project. *The Little Old Sod Shanty* can supplement lesson plans in environmental awareness and agriculture trends. If your class is doing *El Paseo del Vaquero* in conjunction with an area study of the southwestern United States, feel free to have the characters speak a few additional lines of Spanish and decorate the set with southwestern architecture and plants. Each play has enough real-life historical and cultural references to support a host of pre- or post-play activities that integrate easily with related curriculum areas.

Besides those children enrolled in the onstage cast, others can be included in the production as lighting and sound technicians, prop masters, script coaches and stage managers. *Plays of the Wild West* is an excellent vehicle for getting other members of the school and community involved in your project. Maybe there is a Native American dance troupe or an accomplished performer of cowboy songs in your area; ask them to give a special concert/lecture when you present the play. Perhaps someone at your local historical society or library can give a talk about early American transportation for *Pony Express Rider*; a geology professor at a nearby college could add details about 19th-century mining operations for *Klondike Fever*; is there someone at the art museum knowledgeable about George Catlin and other Western illustrators? Try utilizing the talents of local school or youth orchestra members to play incidental music…get the school art club to paint scrims and backdrops…see if a senior citizens' group might volunteer time to sew costumes…inquire whether an Asian restaurant might bring samples of Chinese cuisine for *The Golden Spike*.

Most of all, have lots of fun. Realizing that many performing groups may have limited technical and space resources, I have kept sets, costumes and props minimal. However, if you do have the ability to rig up an entire Navajo village for *The Rainbow Cradle* or build a facsimile *voyageur* canoe for *Bird Woman of the Shoshones*—go for it! Adding more music and dance and visual arts and crafts into the production involves more children and makes your play a genuinely multi-media event.

Similarly, I have supplied only basic stage and lighting directions. Blocking is really the province of the director; once you get the play up and moving, feel free to suit cast and action to your available population and experience level of actors. When figuring out how to stage these plays, I suggest you follow the venerable UYI Method—Use Your Imagination. If the play calls for a boat, bring in a wood frame, an old bathtub or have children draw a boat and hang as a scrim behind where the actors perform. Keep in mind the spirit of the old Andy Hardy musicals: "C'mon, everybody! Let's make a show!"

Age and gender. Obviously, your purpose in putting on the play is to entertain as well as educate; even though in the historical reality of 1869 a Union Pacific tracklaying crew would have been all male, there is no reason these roles can't be played in *your* production by females. After all, the essence of the theatrical experience is to suspend us in time and ask us to believe that anything may be possible. Once again, UYI! Adult characters, such as grandparents or "old mountain men" or "bearded fiddlers," can be played by children costumed or made up to fit the part as closely as possible, or they can actually be played by adults. While *Plays of the Wild West* are intended to be performed chiefly by children, moderate adult involvement will add validation and let children know this isn't just a "kid project." If you want to get very highly choreographed or musically intensive, you will probably find a strategically placed onstage adult or two very helpful in keeping things moving smoothly. Still, *never* underestimate the capacity for even the youngest children to amaze you with their skill and ingenuity in making a show blossom.

Integrating authentic ethnic or period music is a great way to enhance your production. If you have questions about where to find recordings or written music of the tunes or genres included in these plays, or want some tips on performing and arranging them, I would be happy to assist you and may be reached by calling Smith & Kraus, Inc. at their toll-free customer service number, 800-895-4331.

Plays of the Wild West offers the opportunity to learn a little bit more about all of us who make up this amazing nation called the United States of America. So, shine up your spurs, give your lassos a twirl and get ready for some double-barreled, two-fisted, bronc-bustin' action. Happy trails!

L.E. McCullough, Ph.D.
Humanities Theatre Group
Indiana University-Purdue University at Indianapolis
Indianapolis, Indiana

ANNIE OAKLEY: LITTLE SURE-SHOT

Though Annie Oakley (1860–1926) was born in the East, she achieved worldwide renown as a living legend of the Wild West. She surmounted poverty and illiteracy to become by age thirty one of the most well-known women in the world, due to her remarkable skill as a sharpshooter with Buffalo Bill's Wild West Show. Always confident in her own ability, Annie excelled at a time when most women had few opportunities to succeed on their own in public life. And while Annie traveled the world and met kings and queens of many nations, she never forgot her humble beginnings; to the end of her life she retained a strong affection for her family and hometown friends.

TIME: July 25, 1900

PLACE: Greenville, Ohio—Buffalo Bill's Wild West Show

CAST: 28 actors, min. 6 boys, 6 girls

Annie Oakley (Age 40)	Annie Oakley (Age 11–25)
Dervilla	Daniel
Constable	Announcer
Frank Butler	Buffalo Bill Cody
Emily Moses	Annie's Mother
Lyda Stein	Joe Stein
Charlie Stuttelberger	Sitting Bull
3 Cowboys	3 Indians
3 Vaqueros	3 Hecklers
Mayor of Greenville	Photographer

RUNNING TIME: 25 minutes

STAGE SET: a table, a chair, shooting gallery counter, wooden horse

PROPS: hand mirror, comb, old musket, 2 modern rifles, knitting needles, dead squirrel, 3 quarters, 6 stuffed animals, 3 lariats, 3 six-shooters, 3 tomahawks, 6 playing cards, dime, silver trophy cup, old-time box camera with tripod

EFFECTS: Sound—cheering crowd noise; gun shots; gong; bass drum; Visual—camera flash

MUSIC: *Molly Malone, I'll Befriend You* (with bass drum)

COSTUMES: Annie Oakley at Age 40 and performing in the Wild West show wears Stetson hat, calico blouse covered with medals, pleated skirt and gaiters; the younger Annie Oakley dresses as a typical rural teen of the 1870s; Buffalo Bill Cody dresses in his standard Wild West costume: fringed brown buckskin jacket and white pants, long brown or black knee boots, large grey Stetson and a flowing mane and goatee; Sitting Bull wears his full Sioux regalia; other characters dress according to occupation and social station

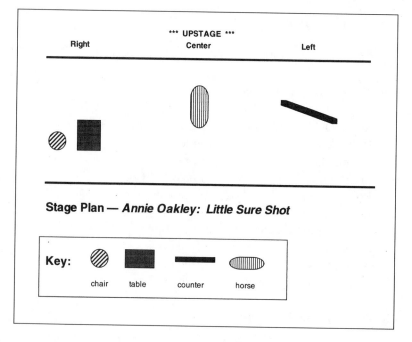

(SOUND: crowd noise up as LIGHTS FADE UP RIGHT on Present-day Annie Oakley sitting at table down right, combing her hair with the aid of a hand mirror; she faces stage left. Two children, Daniel and Dervilla, enter from right and peek cautiously around the curtain at Annie Oakley, edging onstage and whispering. Annie notices but does not turn; crowd noise fades out.)

DANIEL: Hot swallowin' toad frogs, it's *her!*

DERVILLA: Are you sure? Is it her? Are you *really* sure?

DANIEL: Sure as whiskers on a wildcat—that's Annie Oakley!

(A Constable enters from right behind Daniel and Dervilla and frowns, rolls up sleeves.)

ANNIE OAKLEY: *(whirls and points her comb in "shooting" gesture at Daniel and Dervilla)* Smile when you say that, pardners!

(Daniel and Dervilla are startled and jump back into the hands of the Constable, who grabs them by their collars.)

CONSTABLE: Enough of that, you hooligans! What are you doing backstage?

DERVILLA: We didn't mean any harm, constable! Honest!

DANIEL: We just came to see Annie Oakley!

CONSTABLE: You and twenty thousand others—all of whom are in their seats, where *you* should be!

ANNIE OAKLEY: *(laughs)* It's all right. You can let them go. I'll be going on in a minute, anyway.

(Constable releases children.)

CONSTABLE: You pettifoggers are lucky she didn't have a real gun. They don't call her Little Sure-Shot for nothing! *(exits right)*

DANIEL: *(to Dervilla)* Gee willikers, Dervilla! Wouldn't that have been swell? Getting blasted by Annie Oakley!

DERVILLA: Daniel Chambers! Excuse him, Miss Oakley, he's my brother, Daniel, and he's awful dense sometimes. It was *he* who said we should spy on you.

DANIEL: Was not! *(points to Dervilla)* *She* was the one! *She* says she's going to grow up and shoot like Annie Oakley someday! Ha! Fat chance!

ANNIE OAKLEY: I suppose there are worse things to wish for. *(to Dervilla)* What's your name, young miss?

DERVILLA: Er...Miss Chambers, ma'am.

ANNIE OAKLEY: Your *first* name, dear.

DERVILLA: *(hesitates, then whispers)* Dervilla.

DANIEL: Dervilla gorilla! Dervilla gorilla! Dervilla gorilla!

ANNIE OAKLEY: Hush your horns, Mister Soaplock! *(to Dervilla)* Dervilla is a beautiful name and one to be proud of. It's Irish and means "true desire." My husband, Frank, is from Ireland, you know.

DERVILLA: I didn't know that, Miss Oakley.

ANNIE OAKLEY: *(chuckles)* And I bet you didn't know my real name isn't Annie Oakley.

(SOUND: crowd noise up as LIGHTS FADE OUT.)

ANNOUNCER (O.S.) Ladies and gentlemen of Greenville, Ohio! Welcome to the one and only Buffalo Bill Wild West Show, the world's biggest assembly of cowboys and Indians, badmen and outlaws, scouts and rough riders, cyclones, cattle stampedes and other wonders of the Western Frontier! And now Buffalo Bill Cody proudly presents the lovely lass of the Western Plains, Little Sure-Shot—Miss Annie Oakley!

(Crowd noise fades out; SOUND: a single gun shot sounds offstage. LIGHTS UP RIGHT on Annie's Mother, knitting at the table down right; Emily Moses dashes onstage from left.)

EMILY MOSES: Mother! Mother! Phoebe has killed another squirrel! Oh, we can eat supper tonight! *(does a little dance of joy and falls at her mother's feet)*

ANNIE'S MOTHER: *(shudders)* It makes me nervous when she shoots that old blunderbuss. Why, it's 1871, isn't it? Hardly proper for a young girl to be traipsing through the woods all day with a gun on her shoulder!

(Young Annie Oakley enters from left with a dead squirrel and an old musket; Emily rises and takes the musket.)

YOUNG ANNIE OAKLEY: I wish father were alive to see the good use we are making of his rifle.

ANNIE'S MOTHER: He would be ashamed to see his 11-year-old daughter carrying on so! Phoebe Ann Moses, I believe you enjoy shooting that awful weapon!

YOUNG ANNIE OAKLEY: *(puts down squirrel on table)* Mother, you know I do not relish killing. But we have five hungry children and live in the middle of a forest. How else can we survive?

EMILY MOSES: If Phoebe wasn't selling the extra game she shot to the grocer in Greenville, we'd be starving!

ANNIE'S MOTHER: *(sighs)* I suppose you are right. But Phoebe: promise me someday that you will put down that rifle and go to school. Please, Phoebe, promise!

YOUNG ANNIE OAKLEY: I promise, mother! But I don't want to be called Phoebe anymore! From now on, my name is Annie!

(She grabs rifle and storms offstage left; LIGHTS OUT RIGHT.)

ADULT ANNIE OAKLEY (O.S.): I continued to hunt and earn my family food and money until I was fifteen. Then I moved downstate to Cincinnati and lived with my older sister Lyda and her husband Joe Stein. I had decided it was time to go to school and be educated, so I could be a proper young lady like my mother wished. Shortly after I arrived, Lyda and Joe took me to a carnival on the heights overlooking the Ohio River—and my life changed forever.

(LIGHTS UP CENTER on Lyda Stein and Joe Stein walking arm-in-arm, Young Annie tagging behind them, staring at the wonders around her.)

YOUNG ANNIE OAKLEY: The city looks so beautiful from up here! Like a string of pearls shining along the dark ribbon of water!

LYDA STEIN: It does, indeed. Joe and I were thinking of moving from town to one of the new suburbs.

JOE STEIN: They have some wonderful new neighborhoods— Hyde Park, Mount Airy, Oakley.

YOUNG ANNIE OAKLEY: I think you should move to Oakley.

LYDA STEIN: Oakley? Why?

YOUNG ANNIE OAKLEY: I like the sound of it. Fresh, but strong. Oakley is a good name.

JOE STEIN: We will keep it mind. *(points to mid left)* Look, there is Charlie Stuttelberger's Shooting Club! What do you say, Annie? Let us try our luck!

(LIGHTS UP LEFT on Charlie Stuttelberger behind the shooting gallery counter; Joe, Lyda and Annie approach.)

CHARLIE STUTTELBERGER: Step right up, folks, and try your skill at sharpshooting! Anyone can try! Only six shots for a quarter! *(notices Steins)* Well, if it isn't Joe and Lyda Stein! Guten tag! Guten tag! *(shakes hands with Joe and Lyda, bows to Annie)* And who is this pretty young lady?

LYDA STEIN: Charlie Stuttelberger, this is my sister, Annie—

YOUNG ANNIE OAKLEY: Oakley. Annie Oakley. *(shakes Charlie's hand, curtseys)*

CHARLIE STUTTELBERGER: Pleased to make your acquaintance, fraulein Oakley.

JOE STEIN: *(gives two quarters to Charlie)* Hand me a rifle, Charlie. I am loaded for bear!

(Charlie hands Joe a rifle and Joe turns to face center stage.)

JOE STEIN: Now, Annie, here is what you do. See those metal ducks and rabbits moving on that track? If you hit one, you win a prize.

YOUNG ANNIE OAKLEY: What happens if I hit them all?

(Joe, Lyda and Charlie laugh heartily.)

CHARLIE STUTTELBERGER: I like this young Annie Oakley very much! She is very funny!

(Joe puts rifle to his shoulder and aims.)

JOE STEIN: Here goes nothing!

(Joe shoots six times and hits the target the final time; SOUND: a gong.)

JOE STEIN: *(hands rifle to Annie)* There you go. Now, don't be discouraged if you don't hit anything.

(Annie aims and pumps off six quick shots, hitting the target each time; SOUND: six gongs.)

CHARLIE STUTTELBERGER: Fraulein! You hit all the targets!
LYDA STEIN: *(hugs Annie)* That is unbelievable, Annie!
YOUNG ANNIE OAKLEY: *(hands rifle to Charlie)* What do I win?
JOE STEIN: *(hands Charlie another quarter)* Another six shots. Take that rifle back, Annie, and shoot again.

(Annie takes the rifle, aims and pumps off six quick shots, hitting the target each time; SOUND: six gongs.)

CHARLIE STUTTELBERGER: Joe, bring this girl back here tomorrow at ten o'clock sharp. There is someone she *must* meet.
JOE STEIN: We will do that, Charlie.

(Annie whispers to Lyda who whispers to Joe.)

JOE STEIN: Oh, about those prizes…
CHARLIE STUTTELBERGER: Ja, prizes!

(Charlie pulls out a half dozen stuffed animals and gives them to Joe who passes them to Lyda who passes them to Annie; LIGHTS OUT. MUSIC: "Molly Malone.")

FRANK BUTLER: *(SINGS)*
  In Dublin's fair city, where the girls are so pretty
  I first set my eyes on sweet Molly Malone
  As she wheeled her wheelbarrow through streets broad and narrow
  Crying, "Cockles and mussels! Alive, alive, oh!"

(LIGHTS UP LEFT on shooting gallery; Charlie Stuttelberger

stands behind the counter, while Frank Butler polishes a rifle.)

FRANK BUTLER: Charlie, you have got to be joking! Frank Butler, the premier exhibition marksman in the country shooting against a fifteen-year-old girl from the backwoods?

CHARLIE STUTTELBERGER: This is no joke, Frank. The girl is unbelievable!

(Young Annie enters from right carrying a rifle.)

CHARLIE STUTTELBERGER: Ah, here she is! Mr. Frank Butler, meet Miss Annie Oakley!

FRANK BUTLER: *(tips hat)* Please to meet you, Miss Oakley.

YOUNG ANNIE OAKLEY: *(curtseys)* Likewise, I'm sure.

CHARLIE STUTTELBERGER: Mr. Butler is one of the greatest sharpshooters in America, Annie. He—

FRANK BUTLER : Let's get this over with, Charlie. *(to Annie)* Have you ever done trapshooting before, miss?

YOUNG ANNIE OAKLEY: No, sir.

FRANK BUTLER: When you're ready, shout "pull," and the operator sends a clay disc into the air. You shoot it. Simple as that. Got it?

YOUNG ANNIE OAKLEY: Yes, sir.

FRANK BUTLER: First one misses and the other hits, match is over.

YOUNG ANNIE OAKLEY: Yes, sir.

FRANK BUTLER: I'll shoot first, then you.

YOUNG ANNIE OAKLEY: Yes, sir.

(Frank Butler faces center stage, raises his rifle to his shoulder.)

FRANK BUTLER: Pull!

(Charlie Stuttelberger pulls and Frank Butler shoots; SOUND: a single gun shot.)

CHARLIE STUTTELBERGER: Hit!

(Annie faces center stage, raises her rifle to her shoulder.)

YOUNG ANNIE OAKLEY: Pull, please!

(Charlie Stuttelberger pulls and Annie shoots; SOUND: a single gun shot.)

CHARLIE STUTTELBERGER: Hit!

(Frank Butler regards Annie with a mixture of curiosity and respect.)

FRANK BUTLER: So, she *can* shoot after all. *(raises rifle)* Pull!

(Charlie Stuttelberger pulls and Annie shoots; SOUND: a single gun shot.)

CHARLIE STUTTELBERGER: Hit!
YOUNG ANNIE OAKLEY: *(raises rifle)* Pull, please!

(Charlie Stuttelberger pulls and Annie shoots; SOUND: a single gun shot.)

CHARLIE STUTTELBERGER: Hit!

(Frank and Annie shoot seven more times in rapid succession, each hitting the target every time with Charlie declaring "Hit!")

FRANK BUTLER: Pull!

(Charlie Stuttelberger pulls and Frank Butler shoots; SOUND: a single gun shot.)

CHARLIE STUTTELBERGER: Miss!
YOUNG ANNIE OAKLEY: Pull, please!

(Charlie Stuttelberger pulls and Annie shoots; SOUND: a single gun shot.)

CHARLIE STUTTELBERGER: Hit! Annie Oakley wins!

FRANK BUTLER: *(shakes Annie's hand)* Good shooting, Miss Oakley. Very good shooting, indeed.

YOUNG ANNIE OAKLEY: *(curtseys)* Thank you, sir. *(raises rifle)* Pull, please!

(Charlie Stuttelberger pulls and Annie shoots; SOUND: a single gun shot.)

YOUNG ANNIE OAKLEY: Pull, please!

(Charlie Stuttelberger pulls and Annie shoots; SOUND: a single gun shot.)

YOUNG ANNIE OAKLEY: Pull, please!

(Charlie Stuttelberger pulls and Annie shoots; SOUND: a single gun shot. LIGHTS OUT.)

ANNIE OAKLEY: *(O.S.)* I shot fifty straight clay discs, all in a row without a single miss. But even though he seemed a little snooty at first, that Frank Butler turned out to be a good sport. In fact, he married me a year later on June 22, 1876. And as the crack sharpshooting team of Butler and Oakley, we toured the whole United States for nine years. I was able to save up plenty of money to send home to my family, and best of all, I finally got an education. Frank was a smart and well-read man, and when we weren't performing, he worked on teaching me to read and write. Finally, in the summer of 1885, we joined the biggest tour in the business: Buffalo Bill Cody's Wild West Show!

(SOUND: crowd noise up as LIGHTS UP CENTER on Three Vaqueros, Three Cowboys and Three Indians at center stage; Vaqueros twirl lariats, Cowboys strut and shoot six-shooters and Indians dance and brandish tomahawks; a wooden horse stands at mid center.)

VAQUEROS: Vamanos! Cuidado! De acuerdo!

COWBOYS: Eee-hah! Ride 'em, cowboy! Reach for the sky, pardner!

INDIANS: Tatara kita-wira! Hawa re-rawira! He-yo!

(Crowd noises fade, Vaqueros, Cowboys, Indians become quiet; SPOTLIGHT LEFT on Buffalo Bill Cody standing at down left.)

BUFFALO BILL CODY: Ladies and gentlemen, as our star attraction, the Wild West show presents the most extraordinary woman sharpshooter in the entire world, the little girl of the Western Plains—Miss Annie Oakley!

(Young Annie Oakley enters from right carrying rifle, while Frank Butler enters from left; she crosses to horse, curtseys, mounts horse and raises rifle as Vaqueros, Cowboys and Indians circle around her; he crosses to mid right, faces her and mimes tossing balls in the air as she mimes shooting them.)

BUFFALO BILL CODY: Watch her shoot glass balls out of the air from the back of a racing pony!

(SOUND: three rapid rifle shots. Frank Butler holds up playing cards.)

BUFFALO BILL CODY: See her shoot the king and queen of hearts right between the eyes!

(SOUND: two rapid rifle shots. Annie turns around and aims rifle over her shoulder while looking into a hand mirror held by an Indian; Frank Butler puts out his right arm, mimes holding a dime between his fingers.)

BUFFALO BILL CODY: See her shoot a hole through a dime—held between her husband's fingertips—while looking backwards through a mirror!

(SOUND: a rifle shot. Frank Butler shows the dime to the audience.)

FRANK BUTLER: Bullseye!

(SOUND: crowd noise up as Young Annie Oakley dismounts, curtseys and stands behind horse with Vaqueros, Cowboys and Indians.)

BUFFALO BILL CODY: Miss Annie Oakley! And now, from the Dakota Territory, the great Sioux warrior chief who defeated the Seventh Cavalry at the Battle of the Little Big Horn—Chief Sitting Bull!

(Crowd noise fades out as Sitting Bull enters from right, plodding to down center, where he stands and stares without expression at the audience; Three Hecklers enter from right and sit and stand at down right, shouting at Sitting Bull.)

HECKLER #1: Murderer! He massacred those soldiers!
HECKLER #2: Killed Custer and every one of his men!
HECKLER #3: Go back home to the reservation!

(Hecklers mime throwing fruit at Sitting Bull.)

HECKLER #1: Have an apple, you bum! It's more than you gave Custer!
HECKLER #2: Yaaaahhh! Go home!
HECKLER #3: Murderer! Get him outa here!

(Sitting Bull remains standing, expressionless and unflinching. Annie runs in front of horse, aims at the Hecklers and fires. SOUND: three rapid rifle shots.)

HECKLER #1: *(leaps back, holds his throat)* She shot the button off my collar!
HECKLER #2: *(leaps back, holds his left arm)* She shot the button off my sleeve!
HECKLER #3: *(springs forward, looks behind himself)* She shot the button off my—button!

(Hecklers dash offstage right; Sitting Bull turns and faces Annie.)

SITTING BULL: *(smiles)* Little Sure-Shot.

(Annie crosses to Sitting Bull and they shake hands; Sitting Bull sings, holding Annie's hand. MUSIC: "I'll Befriend You" with accompaniment on bass drum.)

SITTING BULL: *(SINGS)*
    Ko-la, ta-ku o-te-hi-ka
    I-ma-ku-wa-pi-lo ni-yo-ye
    He-na ko-wo-ki-pi sni
    He-wa-on we-lo

VAQUEROS, COWBOYS & INDIANS: *(SING)*
    Friend, whatever hardships threaten
    If you call me, I'll befriend you
    All enduring fearlessly
    I'll befriend you

(LIGHTS OUT FULL; drum continues.)

ANNIE OAKLEY: *(O.S.)* Sitting Bull left the Wild West show at the end of the tour, and he was killed at Wounded Knee five years later. But he and I were always good friends. In fact, he adopted me as his honorary daughter. And even today, the beautiful song of friendship he sang runs through my mind.

(Drums stop; LIGHTS UP RIGHT on Present-day Annie Oakley sitting at table with Daniel and Dervilla standing on either side of her.)

ANNIE OAKLEY: In 1887 Buffalo Bill's Wild West Show went to Europe, and we performed for Queen Victoria of England and all the crowned heads of Europe. I even shot the tip of a cigarette out of the mouth of Crown Prince Wilhelm of Germany. He is the Kaiser there now.

DANIEL: Gee willikers, Miss Oakley! You sure have had some amazing adventures!

DERVILLA: Even though you were born in a one-room log cabin in the woods, you have become one of the most famous women in the world. Maybe I can make my dream come true someday.

ANNIE OAKLEY: As the great author Mark Twain says, "keep away from people who try to belittle your ambitions...small people always do that, but the really great make you feel that you, too, can become great."

(LIGHTS UP FULL as Mayor of Greenville, Emily Moses, Lyda Stein, Joe Stein, Annie's Mother, Frank Butler, Buffalo Bill Cody and Photographer enter from left and cross to center where they meet Annie, followed by Daniel and Dervilla; Mayor carries a large silver trophy cup, Photographer carries an old-time box camera with tripod.)

ANNIE OAKLEY: Annie! Emily! Lyda!

(Annie embraces her Mother and Sisters; Photographer sets up camera to the left of group and group gathers together to pose for camera, Mayor on one side of Annie, Frank Butler on the other.)

MAYOR: *(presents cup to Annie and reads inscription)* "To Miss Annie Oakley, from Old Home Friends of Greenville, Ohio." We hope you never forget this day!

ANNIE OAKLEY: I will remember it always!

(MUSIC: "Molly Malone.")

FRANK BUTLER: *(SINGS)*
In Dublin's fair city, where the girls are so pretty
I first set my eyes on sweet Annie Oakley

ALL: *(SING)*
As she wheeled her wheelbarrow through streets broad and narrow
Crying, "Cockles and mussels! Alive, alive, oh!"

PHOTOGRAPHER: Everyone look at me and say "butter beans"!

EVERYONE: Butter beans!

(Photographer shoots photo—LIGHTS FLASH ONCE, THEN GO OUT.)

* THE END *

Molly Malone

(traditional, arranged by L.E. McCullough)

In Dub-lin's fair ci-ty, where the girls are so pret-ty I first set my eyes on sweet Mol-ly Ma-lone As she wheeled her wheel-bar-row through streets broad and nar-row Cry-ing, "Cock-les and mus-sels! A-live, a-live, oh!"

I'll Befriend You

(traditional, arranged by L.E. McCullough)

Ko-la, ta-ku o-te-hi-ka I-ma-ku-wa-pi-lo ni-yo-ye He-na ko-wo-ki-pi sni He-wa-on we-lo Friend, what-ev-er hard-ships threa-ten If you call me, I'll be-friend you All en-dur-ing fear-less-ly I'll be-friend you

BIRD WOMAN OF THE SHOSHONES

For many years historians tended to overlook the active role played by the Shoshone girl, Sacajawea*, in assisting the Lewis and Clark expedition of 1804–06. Just as interesting as her adventures on that epic journey, however, are the tales of what happened to her afterwards. Army officer John C. Frémont reports meeting her in 1843 in eastern Colorado, and there are legends that she married a Ute chief in Utah, was befriended by stagecoach robber Henry Plummer in Montana and lived with Comanches in Kansas. In 1860 she appeared at Ft. Bridger and helped negotiate a treaty between the Shoshones and the United States in 1868 that prevented a bloody war. She spent the last years of her life on the Wind River reservation in Wyoming, telling stories to her people and teaching the Shoshone language to whites—just as she had taught Lewis and Clark decades before. The Rev. John Roberts, an Episcopalian minister, presided at her burial, and in 1963 the Wyoming Daughters of the American Revolution erected a monument at her grave site. There are several Western mountain peaks bearing her name, and statues of her are found in St. Louis, Portland and Bismarck.

* pronounced Sa-ca-ja-WE-a

TIME: April 9, 1884

PLACE: Shoshone Reservation, Wind River, Wyoming Territory

CAST: 16 actors, min. 9 boys, 3 girls

Rev. Roberts	Mrs. Keeler
John Blue Crow	Jane White Plume

Sacajawea
William Clark
George Drouillard
Cameâhwait
4 Shoshone Warriors

Meriwether Lewis
Toussaint Charbonneau
Cruzatte
York

RUNNING TIME: 20 minutes

STAGE SET: tombstone at down right reading "Here Lies Sacajawea, Guide"

PROPS: flowers, blanket, baby doll, rifle, knife

MUSIC: *Song of the Bird Woman*

COSTUMES: Rev. Roberts, Mrs. Keeler, John Blue Crow and Jane White Plume dress in 1880s clothes; Lewis and Clark wear c. 1800 U.S. Army uniforms; Charbonneau, Drouillard, Cruzatte and York wear clothes of early 1800s mountain men; Cameâhwait, Warriors and Sacajawea dress in typical Shoshone costume of the period, with Sacajawea wearing a belt of bright blue beads

(LIGHTS UP RIGHT on Rev. Roberts and Mrs. Keeler standing down right in front of a tombstone reading "Here Lies Sacajawea, Guide.")

REV. ROBERTS: April 9, 1884: Brave Sacajawea was buried today... may her wandering soul find eternal peace.

MRS. KEELER: She was born in 1789, the same year George Washington became the first President of the United States. Think what marvels she saw during her lifetime!

(John Blue Crow and Jane White Plume enter from right, each bearing flowers which they lay on ground before tombstone.)

MRS. KEELER: Reverend Roberts, these are two of my students at the reservation school—Jane White Plume and John Blue Crow.

JANE WHITE PLUME: Good evening, Reverend.

JOHN BLUE CROW: Good evening, Reverend.

REV. ROBERTS: Good evening, children. Mrs. Keeler says Sacajawea was related to you.

JOHN BLUE CROW: Yes, she was. Her cousin, Washakie, is our uncle and chief of the Shoshones. All the Shoshone people loved her very much.

MRS. KEELER: Perhaps you can tell the Reverend one of the stories Sacajawea told you about the old days?

JANE WHITE PLUME: Sacajawea had many stories. Her greatest story was the time she helped guide the expedition of Lewis and Clark across the Rocky Mountains to the Pacific Ocean.

(LIGHTS OUT RIGHT, LIGHTS UP CENTER on Sacajawea, Toussaint Charbonneau, Meriwether Lewis and William Clark. Sacajawea sits on blanket rocking her baby to sleep, with the three men standing around her.)

JANE WHITE PLUME: In the winter of 1805, Sacajawea was living at Fort Mandan on the Missouri River in what is now the Territory of North Dakota. She was sixteen years old and lived with her husband, a French Canadian trader named Toussaint

Charbonneau. She had a two-month old baby boy named Pomp, which means "leader" in Shoshone.

JOHN BLUE CROW: Charbonneau had been hired as an interpreter for the expedition of Lewis and Clark. The expedition had been ordered by President Thomas Jefferson to explore the land the United States had bought from Napoleon in the Louisiana Purchase of 1803—827,000 square miles bounded by the Mississippi River, Gulf of Mexico, Rocky Mountains and Canada.

LEWIS: Monsieur Charbonneau, this expedition will search for a water route that can take us from the Mississippi River to the Pacific Ocean. We will be meeting many Indian tribes along the way. We need someone who can speak their tongues.

CHARBONNEAU: My wife, she can speak to Indians. She is Shoshone. Five years ago she was stolen from her people by the Minnetaree tribe. I buy her from them.

CLARK: But she has a small baby. The trip will be very harsh, even for grown men.

CHARBONNEAU: My wife is very strong. Our baby is very strong.

LEWIS: Very well. We will begin our trip in two months. Until then, let your wife teach us the language and customs of her people.

CLARK: What is your wife's name?

SACAJAWEA: Sacajawea. My name…Sacajawea.

LEWIS: Sacajawea. That is a lovely name. What does it mean?

CHARBONNEAU: It means "bird woman." When she was born, a bird landed at her mother's feet. The Shoshone believed it was a sign of good luck.

CLARK: Let us hope it brings good luck to our expedition.

(LIGHTS OUT CENTER.)

JANE WHITE PLUME: In April 7, 1805, the expedition started westward along the Missouri River led by Lewis and Clark, Clark's servant York, two rugged mountain men—George Drouillard and Cruzatte—and Sacajawea and her husband. It was thrilling moment for everyone…they were on the threshold of one of the greatest journeys in history.

(LIGHTS UP CENTER on the expedition sitting in a wedge as

if in a canoe—Sacajawea with Pomp strapped to her back at the head, York and Charbonneau behind her, Lewis and Clark in the next rank, Drouillard and Cruzatte in the final rank; everyone paddles except for Sacajawea, who peers ahead intently and motions directions to the others.)

JOHN BLUE CROW: Sacajawea was excited because she knew she would once again see her tribe. Sitting in the lead canoe with her baby strapped to her back, she guided the expedition up the treacherous river during the day. At night, when the group made camp, she found herbs and flowers that the men could eat.

LEWIS: I say, Captain Clark, this Indian woman has discovered some very tasty spices in the woods: wild artichokes, sunflower roots, strawberries, currants and plums. Our simple fare of meat and bread pudding is greatly improved.

CLARK: She can also name many trees and plants we have never seen. It is like having a botanist on the trip. And she has told us which tribes have been leaving moccasin prints on the river bank.

JANE WHITE PLUME: For even though the explorers saw no one along the way, they knew they were being watched by unseen eyes.

JOHN BLUE CROW: One day in May, a sudden storm blew up and overturned their canoe as they approached a waterfall.

(The canoe occupants fall out and roll over, thrashing about and shouting.)

JANE WHITE PLUME: Lewis and Clark and York got quickly ashore, and the other men managed to set the canoe right. But the precious supplies were in danger of being washed away down the swirling waterfall.

(Lewis, Clark and York stand at mid-left; Charbonneau, Drouillard and Cruzatte are at mid-center paddling frantically to keep the canoe upright; Sacajawea with Pomp strapped to her back is at down center—she is reaching out and snaring supplies as they float by.)

LEWIS: The canoe has taken on too much water. The supplies are washing out over the sides!

CLARK: This is a disaster! We will lose all our charts and medicines!

LEWIS: Cruzatte! Drouillard! Watch out for the supplies!

CLARK: Charbonneau! Steer to the left! The left!

LEWIS: It's no use! They can't hear us above the rushing water! We'll lose everything!

YORK: Look, Captain! Sacajawea is catching the supplies!

CLARK: Good show! Even the baby is making a grab!

LEWIS: York, swim out and help her!

(York dives in, swims to down center and helps catch supplies.)

CLARK: Captain Lewis, I declare, I do not know how we would survive without that woman!

(LIGHTS OUT CENTER.)

JOHN BLUE CROW: A few days later the expedition passed a beautiful stream that went south from the main river. Lewis named it "The Sacajawea" in honor of her quick efforts in saving many of the supplies.

JANE WHITE PLUME: In mid-August, the expedition reached the Three Forks of the Missouri River. This was the exact spot where Sacajawea had been captured by the Minnetaree five years before.

(LIGHTS UP CENTER on Charbonneau, Clark and Sacajawea with Pomp on her back standing at mid-center looking toward audience; Clark carries a rifle.)

CLARK: It has been over a week since Captain Lewis and Drouillard went ahead to scout our path upriver. I hope they have not come to harm.

SACAJAWEA: Shhhhh! *(hushes and crouches, peering around)*

CLARK: *(raises rifle)* What is it? What does she see?

CHARBONNEAU: *(draws knife)* Trouble, maybe.

(LIGHTS FADE UP LEFT on Cameâhwait and Four Shoshone Warriors at down left; Clark points rifle at them.)

CLARK: Are they hostile?
SACAJAWEA: Aiiiiiiiiiii!

(Sacajawea shouts with glee and runs to Cameâhwait, embracing him.)

CHARBONNEAU: It is her tribe! We are safe!

(Lewis and Drouillard enter from left; Clark and Charbonneau meet them at down center.)

LEWIS: The chief is her brother, Cameâhwait. He has offered to sell us food and fresh horses.
CLARK: We are at the edge of the Great Divide. We must now cross the mountains before winter comes.
LEWIS: The Shoshones will guide us to the next river. I'll take Charbonneau and Drouillard and buy the horses and supplies.
CLARK: Excellent. Monsieur Charbonneau?
CHARBONNEAU: Oui, Captain Clark?
CLARK: I suggest you buy an extra horse for your wife. The "Bird Woman" is bringing us a great deal of good luck.

(LIGHTS OUT.)

JOHN BLUE CROW: After many struggles through the mountains—where deep snow had already set in—the expedition reached the Clearwater River, then the Snake River and finally the Columbia River.
JANE WHITE PLUME: They continued to meet many groups of Indians who welcomed them with great friendliness. Captain Clark wrote in his journal that when the Indians saw Sacajawea, they knew the expedition was a peaceful one. Her presence, he believed, kept them from being attacked.

(LIGHTS UP CENTER; York, Charbonneau, Lewis, Clark, Drouillard, Cruzatte and Sacajawea with Pomp strapped to

her back enter on all fours from left and slowly crawl to mid-center, where they turn and face audience.)

JOHN BLUE CROW: In mid-October, 1805, the expedition came to the mouth of the Columbia. The Pacific Ocean lay just over a mountain, and it was at the bottom of this mountain that the men began to build a fort.

JANE WHITE PLUME: A few days after Christmas, some members of the Clatsop tribe told them there was a whale beached on the shore. It took the expedition two days to reach the top of the mountain.

(Sacajawea slowly stands and gazes out at audience.)

JOHN BLUE CROW: When they got there, Sacajawea—with her baby still on her back—stood and looked out at the ocean. She had never seen such a huge body of water.

(Others slowly stand and gaze at audience, pointing.)

JANE WHITE PLUME: She took her baby and held him up to see the marvelous sight.

(Sacajawea holds up baby.)

JANE WHITE PLUME: Years later when he was a grown man, Pomp would tell people that his first memory was of the beautiful blue ocean.

(LIGHTS FADE OUT.)

JOHN BLUE CROW: The Lewis and Clark expedition returned to their starting point at Fort Mandan in August, 1806. They had done what no other white explorers had done—they had crossed half the North American continent, lived with many tribes of Native Americans and discovered new plants and animals, all without losing a single person in the party.

(LIGHTS UP RIGHT on Rev. Roberts, Mrs. Keeler, John Blue Crow and Jane White Plume standing at tombstone.)

MRS. KEELER: Sacajawea brought very good luck to the expedition.

JANE WHITE PLUME: We are proud to have her as an ancestor.

REV. ROBERTS: In the years to come, she will be honored as one of the outstanding women of American history.

JOHN BLUE CROW: Until then, we will honor her with this song, *Bird Woman's Song*. Join us as we sing to a great American explorer.

(MUSIC: "Bird Woman's Song.")

REV. ROBERTS, MRS. KEELER, JANE WHITE PLUME & JOHN BLUE CROW: *(SING)*

Sacajawea, Shoshone maid
Fearless pathfinder, never afraid
Leading the pace to trail's final end
Bird Woman brings good luck to her friends

(Other characters come onstage and sing.)

ALL: *(SING)*

Crossing the Rockies, fording the Snake
Braving vast deserts, adventure to make
Bird Woman guides, her wisdom is strong
Guiding the way with a heart full of song

Sacajawea, Shoshone maid
Fearless pathfinder, never afraid
Leading the pace to trail's final end
Bird Woman brings good luck to her friends

(LIGHTS OUT.)

* THE END *

Bird Woman's Song

(words & music by L.E. McCullough)

Sac- a- ja- we- a, Sho- sho- ne maid

Fear- less path- fin- der, ne- ver a- fraid

Lea- ding the pace to trail's fi- nal end

Bird wo- man brings good luck to her friends

DARLING CLEMENTINE:
A TAIL OF OLD SAN FRANCISCO

The growth of San Francisco, California from a tiny fishing village into one of the grand cities of the world is the story of many bold risk-takers—and many bold lawbreakers. The California Gold Rush of the late 1840s flooded San Francisco with thousands of fortune seekers from around the world, and the city's early history was marked by chaos and lawlessness. Within a few years, however, San Francisco had become a thriving center of industry and commerce as well as a sophisticated breeding ground for great literature, theatre and music, a reputation it still enjoys.

TIME: 1847–1869

PLACE: San Francisco, California

CAST: 34 actors, min. 10 boys, 5 girls

Miss Clementine, a Cat	Mrs. Cuddahy
Newsboy	John Henry Brown
Yerba Buena Man	Yerba BuenaWoman
James Marshall	2 Prospectors
2 Rats	Bystander
Arsonist	3 Firemen
2 Sydney Ducks	Shanghai Chicken
Sailor	Selim Woodworth
4 Vigilantes	Levi Strauss
Mary Ann Magnin	2 Minstrels
Lotta Crabtree	Edwin Booth
Bret Harte	Ambrose Bierce
Mark Twain	

RUNNING TIME: 25 minutes

STAGE SET: sign reading "City Hotel, San Francisco, Calif.—Est. 1847" at down right hanging over a cushion, wood block at down left

PROPS: saucer, newspapers, telescope, notebook, gold pan, gold nugget, shovel, torch, knife, sap, noose rope, proclamation, scissors, blue jeans, measuring tape, lace doily, poem sheet, book, firehose

EFFECTS: Sound—fire bells

MUSIC: *My Darling Clementine*, *Blow the Man Down*, *Turkey in the Straw*

COSTUMES: Miss Clementine wears a cat costume; Rats wear rat masks and tails; John Henry Brown wears mid-19th-century English sailor garb; Yerba Buena Man and Woman dress as Spanish *Californios*; Levi Strauss can wear denim pants and jacket; other characters (Vigilantes, Prospectors, Minstrels, Bret Harte, Mark Twain, etc.) dress in mid-19th-century garb befitting their occupation or status

(LIGHTS UP FULL; at down right lies Miss Clementine, the cat, snoozing comfortably and stretching lazily on a cushion underneath a sign reading "City Hotel, San Francisco, Calif.—Est. 1847." Mrs. Cuddahy warbles "My Darling Clementine" offstage left.)

MRS. CUDDAHY: *(SINGS, O.S.)*
Oh my darling, oh my darling
Oh my darling Clementine!

MISS CLEMENTINE: *(awakes with a start and stares offstage right)* What's all the racket? Can't you see there's a cat sleeping in here?

(Mrs. Cuddahy bustles onstage from left carrying a saucer, stands at center and calls out.)

MRS. CUDDAHY: Cleeeeee-men-tine! Oh, Cleeeeee-men-tine! Here kitty-kitty! Here kitty-kitty! Come out, come out wherever you are!

MISS CLEMENTINE: *(to audience) That* overly cheerful creature is Mrs. Cuddahy, the manager of my hotel. She's generally pleasant—for a human—but I can*not* understand this intrusion into my sleeping quarters. Why, it's not even two o'clock in the afternoon! If I ignore her, she usually goes away.

(Miss Clementine burrows deeper into her cushion, while Mrs. Cuddahy wanders around stage calling out.)

MRS. CUDDAHY: I've got a special treat for you, Clementine. A special treatsie-weetsie for the kitty-witty!

MISS CLEMENTINE: *(perks up, to audience)* Treat? Did she say treat? *(to Mrs. Cuddahy)* Meowwww! Meowwww! *(sits and paws the air)*

MRS. CUDDAHY: Oh, there you are, you silly kittums. I've got a surprise for you-uuuuu!

(Mrs. Cuddahy crosses to Miss Clementine and sets the saucer on the floor in front of the cushion; she pets Miss Clementine's head as the cat laps milk from the saucer.)

MRS. CUDDAHY: There's a good lady-puss.

MISS CLEMENTINE: *(licks lips, nods toward Mrs. Cuddahy)* There's a good human.

MRS. CUDDAHY: Twenty-two years old and still loves her buttermilk.

MISS CLEMENTINE: Don't rub it in! You're no spring kitten yourself, you know! *(to audience)* And that's *Miss* Clementine to you. I may be twenty-two years old, but I still require all the respect you young whelps can muster!

(Newsboy enters from stage left hawking papers.)

NEWSBOY: Extra! Extra! Central Pacific and Union Pacific Railroads meet at Promontory Point, Utah! First railroad link across the entire United States, read all about it! *(exits left)*

MRS. CUDDAHY: Oh, Clementine! Will modern wonders never cease? *(Mrs. Cuddahy starts to exit offstage right, turns and fondly regards Miss Clementine.)* When I came to America from Ireland in 1859, it took me five months to get from Boston to San Francisco by wagon. Now, ten years later, you can make the trip in a week by train!

MISS CLEMENTINE: Humans! *Always* on the move. Of course, that's how *I* got here.

(John Henry Brown enters from left and stands on block at down left, looking through telescope out at audience.)

MISS CLEMENTINE: Twenty-two years ago I was a lonely orphaned kitten on the docks of Liverpool, England. A sailor named John Henry Brown befriended me and took me aboard his ship. We landed in San Francisco the Fourth of July, 1847, a few months after the United States had taken California away from Mexico following the Mexican-American War. Naturally, I thought all the fireworks were celebrating *my* arrival on this new continent.

(Brown steps off block and is greeted warmly by Yerba Buena Man and Woman, who have entered from left; they walk together to center.)

MISS CLEMENTINE: In 1847, of course, the town was still called by the name the original settlers from Mexico had given it— Yerba Buena, which means "good grass" or "good herb" in Spanish. Believe me, this town had *plenty* of fresh catnip and mint grass back then.

(Brown crosses to hotel sign and straightens it.)

MISS CLEMENTINE: Anyway, once landed, my human abandoned his seafaring ways and built this hotel, the City Hotel, at Clay and Kearney Streets...only of course, there were no paved streets here back then.

JOHN HENRY BROWN: *(to Miss Clementine)* Oh, this sleepy little village is going to grow, my frisky young kitten! We'll put down our roots and grow along with it!

YERBA BUENA MAN: *(consults notebook)* According to the official records of 1847, the village of Yerba Buena has 79 buildings, mostly huddled around the waterfront. And there are 459 humans—

YERBA BUENA WOMAN: Of which 128 are females and 273 can read and write—

YERBA BUENA MAN: And including 34 Indians, 38 native Californians, 27 Germans—

YERBA BUENA WOMAN: 22 English, 14 Irish—

YERBA BUENA MAN: 14 Scots, 6 Swiss—

YERBA BUENA WOMAN: 5 Canadians, 10 Africans—

YERBA BUENA MAN: And 40 from the Sandwich Islands.

JOHN HENRY BROWN: A regular Mulligan's stew of humanity!

MISS CLEMENTINE: Throw in a few oysters, and I'd take a bite!

(Brown, Yerba Buena Man and Woman exit right; James Marshall enters from left and sits on block at down left, facing audience and panning for gold.)

MISS CLEMENTINE: *(settles down in cushion, yawns largely)* A few ships came in bearing new settlers, but things were pretty quiet until January 24, 1848. That was the day James Marshall was washing his dirty dishes in the creek at John Sutter's Mill in Coloma, about a hundred miles east of San Francisco.

JAMES MARSHALL: Eurkea! I have found it! *(picks up nugget, shows it to audience)* Gold! Pure, precious gold! Why, the rivers in California are full of gold! *(dashes offstage left)*

MISS CLEMENTINE: You can imagine how well *he* kept a secret.

(Two Prospectors enter from left—one carrying a pan, the other a shovel—and set about digging and panning.)

MISS CLEMENTINE: The California Gold Rush was on, and hundreds of thousands of humans dazzled by dreams of wealth flocked to California from everywhere in the world—three thousand of them lived in tents right here in the city. By the fall of 1849 over 800 ships were anchored in San Francisco Bay. Often the crews jumped ship and ran off to the gold fields.

(Two Rats scurry onstage from left, giggling as they skitter to a stop to the left of Miss Clementine.)

MISS CLEMENTINE: And the rats they brought jumped ship, too, following *their* humans onto land. *(hisses, arches back at Rats, slashes out with paw)* Mrrrowwww!

(Rats gasp, clutch hearts and crawl offstage right.)

MISS CLEMENTINE: Whew! Was I ever a busy mouser in those years! They could have called it the California Rat Rush, as far as I was concerned. *(licks lips)* Mmmm-mmmm-mmmm…

(MUSIC: Prospector #1 begins singing "My Darling Clementine.")

PROSPECTOR #1: *(SINGS)*
Oh my darling, oh my darling
Oh my darling Clementine!

MISS CLEMENTINE: Mrrroowww! *(hisses, arches back)* I *detest* that song! *(to audience)* Do you want to know something? Clementine isn't my real name. My real *cat* name is Princess Jezzabel Dauphine Pangur Ban Crossbow, descendant of fierce Iruscan of ancient Ireland, the King of Cats, and the beautiful

Queen Li Chou Khan of Persia. But my human, Brown, heard this silly song and thought it was just the name for me! Listen to that caterwauling! *(sighs)* Humans! Can't live with 'em, can't eat 'em! *(puts paws over her ears while Prospectors sing discordantly)*

PROSPECTOR #2: *(SINGS)*
> In a cavern in a canyon
> Excavating for a mine
> Dwelt a miner, forty-niner
> And his daughter Clementine

PROSPECTORS #1 & 2: *(SING)*
> Oh my darling, oh my darling
> Oh my darling Clementine!
> She is lost and gone forever
> Dreadful sorry, Clementine!

(Prospectors exit left; Miss Clementine uncovers her ears.)

MISS CLEMENTINE: California grew so much in the next few years, it was admitted as the thirty-first state of the union on September 9, 1850. San Francisco was growing, too. By 1850, more than 800 Chinese had settled along Sacramento Street and founded Chinatown. The Germans gathered at the end of Mongtomery Street and the Irish around St. Patrick's Church. The Jews built their first synagogue, Sherith Israel, on Stockton Street, and a contingent of Australians were hunkered down in a section called Sydney Town—more on them later.

(A Bystander runs onstage from left, stands at center and points to audience.)

BYSTANDER: Fire! Fire! Fire in Denison's Exchange!

(Arsonist carrying torch enters from behind curtain at up right, makes lighting motions around up and mid stage, before sneaking offstage right. SOUND: Fire bells ringing. Three Firemen pulling a hose enter from left, guided by Bystander directing them to point hose at audience.)

MISS CLEMENTINE: Between December, 1849 and June, 1851, there were six major fires in San Francisco. Over twenty-five million dollars in damage was caused and hundreds of buildings were destroyed. The fires spread so easily because most of the buildings were made of wood—even the sidewalks were made of wooden planks. A recent arrival from Pennsylvania, Robert La Motte, wrote to friends back home:

BYSTANDER: Almost without exception the firemen here are gentlemen, and almost every gentlemen in town is a fireman. I never saw any men work as well and as hard as they do here at a fire, fearing nothing and caring for nothing but stopping the destruction.

(Firemen control fire, wind up hose and exit right followed by Bystander.)

MISS CLEMENTINE: I don't mind telling you, I had my whiskers singed on more than one occasion!

(Two Sydney Ducks loiter onstage from left; #1 sits on the wooden block, cleaning nails with a long knife, #2 rubs his hands along a sap.)

MISS CLEMENTINE: Remember that neighborhood I mentioned called Sydney Town? Well, in the 1850s it was no place for a lady—or most men, either. As soon as word of the Gold Rush got out, escaped convicts from the Australian prison colonies at Sydney hurried to San Francisco to take advantage of the loose money the miners were throwing around. They were called the Sydney Ducks, and they ran dozens of gang clubs that murdered and stole from honest citizens. It was robbers from Sydney Town, in fact, who started the great fires in order to cover up their crimes.

(Sailor enters from right, swaying a bit, tips cap to Miss Clementine as he crosses unsteadily toward center stage, drawing the attention of the Syndey Ducks, who hide their weapons and saunter to meet him at center, singing "Blow the Man Down.")

SYNDEY DUCKS #1 & 2: *(SING)*
    Come all you young fellows that follow the sea
    To me way, hey, blow the man down
    Now please pay attention and listen to me
    Give me some time to blow the man down

(The Sydney Ducks flank the Sailor, joshing with him, as Shanghai Chicken enters from left and crosses to center, regarding them somberly and brandishing his hooked hand.)

MISS CLEMENTINE: The favorite crime of the Sydney Ducks was "crimping" sailors. They'd pretend they were a sailor's friend, then knock him over the head and sell him to a ship in the harbor. The next thing the poor sailor knew, he was a slave on the high seas. So many of these sailors ended up on ships bound for the port of Shanghai in China, people said they got "shanghaied." And the worst of the kidnappers were nicknamed that, too—Shanghai Brown, Shanghai Kelly and the very *very* worst, Shanghai Chicken, who had a hook for a left hand.

(Shanghai Chicken, humming "Blow the Man Down," approaches Sydney Ducks and Sailor.)

SHANGHAI CHICKEN: Ahoy there, mate! Welcome to San Francisco. How would you like a nice plate of Chinese food?
SAILOR: Chinese food? That would taste delicious!

(Sydney Duck #2 hits Sailor on head with sap; Sailor falls into arms of Sydney Duck #1, who drags him offstage left, followed by Sydney Duck #2 and Shanghai Chicken.)

SHANGHAI CHICKEN: Well then you can have some—in China!
    (laughs wickedly and exits, humming "Blow the Man Down")

(Selim Woodworth and Four Vigilantes enter from right, Woodworth holding a proclamation, Vigilante #1 holding a noose rope.)

MISS CLEMENTINE: The Sydney Ducks and other criminals

became so bold, the law-abiding citizens of San Francisco took the law into their own hands. In June, 1851, after the sixth terrible fire had swept the city, a Vigilance Committee was organized with over five hundred members. Selim Woodworth was their leader.

SELIM WOODWORTH: *(reads proclamation to audience)* Whereas it has become apparent to the Citizens of San Franciso that there is no security for life and property under the laws as now administered, therefore the Citizens whose names are hereunto attached do unite themselves into an association for the maintenance of the peace and good order of Society.

(Vigilantes #2, 3 and 4 dash offstage left and drag out the Two Sydney Ducks, marching them to center where Vigilante #1 hangs them.)

MISS CLEMENTINE: The Vigilance Committee hung John Jenkins, a thief, James Stuart, a murderer, and two other criminals and closed down most of the gang clubs in Sydney Town. The Vigilance Committee disbanded, too, though crime got so bad five years later, they had to re-form and clean house again.

(Vigilantes drag dead Sydney Ducks offstage left, followed by Woodworth.)

MISS CLEMENTINE: But folks in San Francisco made money in honest ways, too.

(Levi Strauss enters from right with scissors and blue jeans.)

MISS CLEMENTINE: Levi Strauss was born in Bavaria, Germany and came to San Francisco in 1850 to join the Gold Rush. He was a dry goods dealer who wanted to sell cloth to miners so they could make tents.

LEVI STRAUSS: *(to Miss Clementine)* By the time I arrived, the miners had all the tents they needed. But they did not have durable work clothes. So I took my cloth and made pants and shirts instead of tents. *(chuckles)* "Levis," they call them. I think they're going to be very popular for a long time to come.

(Levi Strauss exits right, passing Mary Ann Magnin who enters from right with measuring tape and a lace doily.)

MISS CLEMENTINE: And you've heard of the I. Magnin fine clothing stores? They are all around the country. Well, they were started by Isaac Magnin, who came here from England with his wife, Mary Ann, a most excellent seamstress.

MARY ANN MAGNIN: *(places doily on Miss Clementine's cushion)* There you go, darling Clementine. A beautiful bit of lace to match your beautiful fur. *(exits right)*

MISS CLEMENTINE: *(to audience)* I quite agree. *(sniffs air)* Mmmmm...smell that coffee? Hills Brothers on Sansome Street and J.A. Folger over on California Street started here. So did R.H. Macy, founder of the world's greatest department store. And after a while people learned how to take better care of their money, sending it with the Western Union telegraph company or keeping it in a Wells Fargo bank.

(Two Minstrels enter from left, dancing to center. MUSIC: "Turkey in the Straw.")

MISS CLEMENTINE: But the folks I liked best were the entertainers. From the very start San Francisco has been filled with some of the greatest musicians and dancers and actors in the entire world. They had grand opera houses with opera companies from French, Italy and England. There was a Chinese orchestra at the Adelphi Theatre. And the leading minstrel troupe of the day, the famous Bryant and Christy Minstrels.

(Minstrels step to edge of stage and sing to audience. MUSIC: "Turkey in the Straw.")

MINSTREL #1: *(SINGS)*
Well, I hitched up the wagon and I drove it down the road
With a two-horse wagon and a four-horse load

MINSTREL #2: *(SINGS)*
> "Crack!" went the whip, and the lead horse sprung
> And I said goodbye to the wagon tongue

MINSTREL #1: *(SINGS)*
> Turkey in the hay!

MINSTREL #2: *(SINGS)*
> Hay-hay-hay!

MINSTREL #1: *(SINGS)*
> Turkey in the straw!

MINSTREL #2: *(SINGS)*
> Haw-haw-haw!

MINSTRELS #1 & 2: *(SING)*
> Pick em up, shake em up, anyway at all
> And strike up a tune called "Turkey in the Straw"

(Minstrels exit left; Lotta Crabtree and Edwin Booth enter from right and cross to center.)

MISS CLEMENTINE: And talk about theatre! It was everywhere you turned. Lola Montez, Edwin Forrest, Laura Keene—who played before President Lincoln the night he died—and my personal favorites, Lotta Crabtree and Edwin Booth, performing excerpts from *A Live Woman in the Mines* by Alonzo Delano, written in 1857.

LOTTA CRABTREE: Oh, John, I am tired almost to death! I have been walking all day, inquiring for a situation at every respectable house, without success.

EDWIN BOOTH: Here in this land of gold, amidst the splendor of wealth, we are indeed beggars. *(clasps her hand)* As we have lived together, so shall we die!

LOTTA CRABTREE: Talk not of death, dear husband, for till the breath is out of the body, nobody in California dies. We will succeed! *(points offstage right)* Look, there is our friend, Pike County Jess, with news of our mine claim!

(Lotta takes Edwin by the hand and leads him offstage right; Edwin stops at Miss Clementine.)

EDWIN BOOTH: Yes, but first we must pay homage to this most noble of creatures, The Cat.
(Lotta and Edwin pet Miss Clementine, then exit offstage right.)

MISS CLEMENTINE: A masterful performance!

(Bret Harte, Mark Twain and Ambrose Bierce enter from left, cross to center and face audience.)

MISS CLEMENTINE: Oh, and the writers really made me purr! By the middle of the 1860s, San Francisco was a literary capital. There was the novelist and poet Bret Harte.

(Bret Harte takes a step forward, reads from a poem sheet.)

BRET HARTE:
"San Francisco—From the Sea"
Serene, indifferent of Fate
Thou sittest at the Western Gate

Upon they height, so lately won
Still slant the banners of the sun

Thou seest the white seas strike their tents
O Warder of two Continents

Then rise, O Fleecy Fog, and raise
The glory of her coming days

When forms familiar shall give place
To stranger speech and newer face

(Bret Harte bows to audience, steps back; Ambrose Bierce steps forward.)

MISS CLEMENTINE: Ambrose Bierce was a newspaperman who wrote a humor column in the *San Francisco Examiner*.
AMBROSE BIERCE: The Definition of Positive, an adjective—"to be mistaken at the top of one's voice." The Definition of a Clarinet—"an instrument of torture operated by a person with

cotton in his ears. There are two instruments worse than a clarinet—two clarinets."

(Ambrose Bierce bows to audience, steps back; Mark Twain steps forward.)

MISS CLEMENTINE: And my very favorite author of early San Francisco, Mark Twain. He went to the mining camps and wrote his first short story, "The Celebrated Jumping Frog of Calaveras County."

MARK TWAIN: Well, this here Smiley ketched a frog one day and took him home and said he calculated to educate him. And you bet he did learn him, too! He'd give him a little punch behind, and the next minute you'd see that frog whirling in the air like a donut—see him turn a somersault, or maybe a couple if he got a good start, and come down flat-footed and all right, like a cat. *(looks at Miss Clementine, who sniffs)* Smiley said all a frog wanted was education and he could do most anything. And when it come to fair and square jumping on a dead level, he could get over more ground at one straddle than any animal of his breed. "What's he good for?" asked the stranger. "He's good enough for one thing," Smiley says. "He can out-jump any frog in Calaveras County."

(Mark Twain bows to audience and Harte, Twain and Bierce bow to Miss Clementine, then turn and exit left.)

MISS CLEMENTINE: *(to audience)* It's so nice to have clever friends. *(stretches)* My, all that excitement has made me drowsy. Time for a catnap.

MRS. CUDDAHY: *(SINGS, O.S.)*
Oh my darling, oh my darling
Oh my darling Clementine!

MISS CLEMENTINE: *(grimaces)* Mrrrow! There's that infernal racket again. What's a respectable feline to do? I'll just dream of smoked salmon for supper. Or fresh oysters. Or maybe a nice serving of mackerel. San Francisco is a great city for seafood, you know. And whatever food this kitten sees, she eats. Pleasant dreams! *(settles into cushion and snoozes)*

MRS. CUDDAHY: *(SINGS, O.S.)*
    She is lost and gone forever
    Dreadful sorry, Clementine!

(LIGHTS OUT.)

* THE END *

My Darling Clementine

(traditional, arranged by L.E. McCullough)

In a cav- ern in a can- yon ex- ca- va- ting for a mine Dwelt a mi- ner, for- ty- ni- ner and his daugh- ter Cle- men- tine Oh my dar- ling, oh my dar- ling oh my dar- ling Cle- men- tine! She is lost and gone for- e- ver dread- ful sor- ry, Cle- men- tine!

Blow the Man Down

(traditional, arranged by L.E. McCullough)

Come all you young fel- lows that fol- low the sea, To me way, hey, blow the man down! Now please pay at- ten- tion and lis- ten to me Give me some time to blow the man down

Turkey in the Straw
(traditional, arranged by L.E. McCullough)

Well, I hitched up the wa- gon and I drove it down the road with a

two- horse wa- gon and a four- horse load; "Crack!" went the whip, and the

lead horse sprung and I said good- bye to the wa- gon tongue

Tur- key in the hay! Hay- hay- hay! Tur- key in the straw!

Haw- haw- haw! Pick 'em up, shake 'em up, a- ny- way at all and

strike up a tune called "Tur- key in the Straw"

"GIT ALONG, LITTLE DOGIES!"

Git Along, Little Dogies is perhaps the most widely known and best-loved cowboy song of all time. According to the early 20th-century folksong collector, John A. Lomax, who printed it in his *Cowboy Songs* of 1910, the term "dogie" was a cowboy term describing a motherless calf forced to eat grass before it was old enough to digest it, hence developing a big stomach from malnutrition. Much of cowboy "lingo" derived from specialized terms related to their work, and many of those words came from Spanish—the language of the first American cattle drivers, the *vaqueros*. *La reata* (the rope) became "lariat," *lazo* (slipknot) became "lasso," *chaparejos* (breeches) became "chaps," *pintar* (to paint) became "pinto," a painted horse, and *rodear*—a verb meaning to encircle or surround—became the English "rodeo."

TIME: March, 1871

PLACE: San Saba, Texas

CAST: 16–22 actors, min. 6 boys, 2 girls

Jake	Jenny
Aunt Laura	Ramon Diego
Harvey Coryell	Crawfish Charlie
Jesse Chisholm	Joseph McCoy
Army Officer	6-12 Cattle
Railroad Engineer	

RUNNING TIME: 15 minutes

STAGE SET: a stool, a counter, hanging sign or banner behind counter that reads: "San Saba General Store—Mrs. L. Curtin,

Prop.," two scrims depicting scenes of the Chisholm Trail and the Abilene Stockyards

PROPS: men's work shirt, pinto beans, bean container, chalk, blackboard slate, supply list, blueprints, basket, large spoon, frying pan, packets of flour, cornmeal, salt and sugar

MUSIC: *Git Along, Little Dogies*, *Soy Pobre Vaquero*, *The Old Chisholm Trail*

COSTUMES: all characters dress in post-Civil War Western clothes; Crawfish Charlie wears a white apron, a bandana around his head; Jesse Chisholm, Harvey Coryell and Ramon Diego should wear working cowboy clothes with leg chaps, boots and spurs, wide-brimmed hats; Joseph McCoy wears a suit; Army Officer wears a Civil War-era army uniform; Railroad Engineer dresses in overalls and peaked railroad cap; Cattle wear cattle masks and brown pajamas or sweatsuits and crawl on hands and knees while being herded

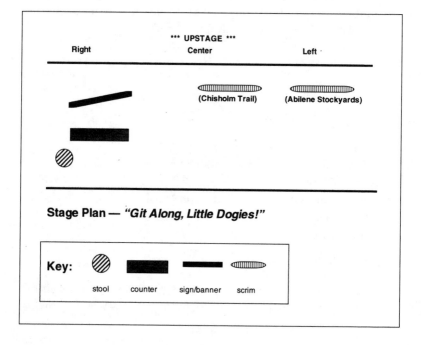

(LIGHTS UP FULL. At down right Jake and Jenny assist their Aunt Laura in the family general store. Aunt Laura stands behind the counter folding a men's work shirt; Jenny stands next to her pouring pinto beans into a container; Jake sits on a stool in front of the counter, writing with chalk on a blackboard slate.)

AUNT LAURA: Did your teacher give you extra homework, Jake?

JAKE: No, Aunt Laura. I am just practicing my letters on my own. *(holds up slate for Aunt Laura to see)*

AUNT LAURA: *(looks askance at slate, frowns)* That is lovely writing. But what language is it?

JENNY: It is a cattle brand—the Circle Bar T. That is the ranch Mister Tuttle owns just outside of town.

AUNT LAURA: I thought you were going to grow up to be President, Jake.

JAKE: Oh, I suppose I will, after President Grant retires. But first, I think I might like to go on a cattle drive to Kansas.

JENNY: Father says I can go along, too, if I learn my multiplication tables up to ten times ten.

(MUSIC: the first phrase of "Git Along, Little Dogies" played offstage. Two cowboys, Ramon Diego and Harvey Coryell, enter from down left and stride over to Jenny, Jake and Aunt Laura.)

HARVEY CORYELL: *(tips hat)* Howdy, ma'am, children. My name is Harvey Coryell.

RAMON DIEGO: *(takes off hat, bows)* Buenas tardes, señora y señorita y señor. Mi nombre es Ramon Diego.

AUNT LAURA: Good afternoon, gentlemen. Welcome to the San Saba General Store. How can we help you?

HARVEY CORYELL: We are about to join up with the cattle drive to Abilene.

RAMON DIEGO: It is a very long trip. We need many supplies.

AUNT LAURA: Well, you have come to the right place. Give me your list, and I will get them all for you.

(Ramon Diego hands Aunt Laura a piece of paper; she exits up right.)

JENNY: How many cattle are you taking?

HARVEY CORYELL: Close to three thousand head. We will travel an average of twelve miles a day.

RAMON DIEGO: Which means if we start on April first, it will take almost six months for us to arrive in Abilene, Kansas from here in Texas.

JAKE: What trail do you take to Abilene?

HARVEY CORYELL: We will take the Old Chisholm Trail.

JENNY: I have heard of that trail. Wasn't it made by a man named Jesse Chisholm?

RAMON DIEGO: You are right, muchacha. Jesse Chisholm was born in Tennessee.

(Jesse Chisholm enters from down left and stands for a moment facing audience as if looking at the trail ahead. He is joined by an Army Officer from down left; they confer briefly and Chisholm turns left and waves forward the rest of his party—a herd of longhorn Cattle. During the song, the Cattle crawl upstage and are herded offstage up center by Chisholm and the Army Officer, who also exit.)

RAMON DIEGO: His father was from Scotland, and his mother was a Cherokee Indian. He first drove cattle through Texas for the United States army in the 1840s. After the Civil War, he started to bring cattle north to Kansas.

HARVEY CORYELL: Here is a song we cattle drivers sing about that trail. It is called *The Old Chisholm Trail.*

(Harvey Coryell and Ramon Diego face audience. MUSIC: "The Old Chisholm Trail.")

HARVEY CORYELL: *(SINGS)*
Oh, come along, boys, and listen to my tale
I'll tell you all my troubles on the Old Chisholm Trail

HARVEY CORYELL & RAMON DIEGO: *(SING)*
Come-a ti-yi youpy-youpy-ya youpy-yay
Come-a ti-yi youpy-youpy-yay

HARVEY CORYELL: *(SINGS)*
>I'm up in the morning afore daylight
>And afore I sleep, the moon shines bright

HARVEY CORYELL, RAMON DIEGO, JAKE & JENNY: *(SING)*
>Come-a ti-yi youpy-youpy-ya youpy-yay
>Come-a ti-yi youpy-youpy-yay

HARVEY CORYELL: *(SINGS)*
>It's bacon and beans most every day
>I'd as soon be eating prairie hay

HARVEY CORYELL, RAMON DIEGO, JAKE & JENNY: *(SING)*
>Come-a ti-yi youpy-youpy-ya youpy-yay
>Come-a ti-yi youpy-youpy-yay

HARVEY CORYELL: *(SINGS)*
>I woke up one morning on the Chisholm Trail
>With a rope in my hand and a cow by the tail

HARVEY CORYELL, RAMON DIEGO, JAKE & JENNY: *(SING)*
>Come-a ti-yi youpy-youpy-ya youpy-yay
>Come-a ti-yi youpy-youpy-yay
>Come-a ti-yi youpy-youpy-ya youpy-yay
>Come-a ti-yi youpy-youpy-yay

JENNY: That is a fine song. But why do ranchers take the cattle to Kansas?

HARVEY CORYELL: To sell them to cattle buyers who send them back East for folks to eat.

JAKE: Don't folks back East have their own cattle?

RAMON DIEGO: No, muchacho, not everyone is as lucky as we are in Texas. People in big cities back East only raise cats and dogs and mosquitoes.

(Joseph McCoy and a Railroad Engineer enter from down left; McCoy carries blueprints, which he unrolls and shows to Railroad Engineer as he gazes out at audience, pointing into the distance.)

HARVEY CORYELL: In 1866 a man from Springfield, Illinois named Joseph McCoy came to Abilene and built a lot of pens to keep cattle in. Then he convinced the Kansas Pacific Railroad to build a train depot, and the cattle were loaded onto trains and shipped back East.

(The herd of longhorn Cattle enter from up center and crawl to down left, where they are herded offstage by McCoy and the Railroad Engineer, who also exit.)

RAMON DIEGO: That first year thirty-five thousand Texas cattle were driven to Abilene, seventy-five thousand the next year. Last year, in 1870, there were over three hundred fifty thousand.

JENNY: That sure is a lot of cattle!

CRAWFISH CHARLIE: *(O.S.)* And I sure am a lot of hungry!

(Crawfish Charlie enters from down left—large spoon in one hand, frying pan on the other—and crosses to center stage as Aunt Laura enters from up right carrying a basket.)

CRAWFISH CHARLIE: Who's got the vittles in this bunkhouse?

AUNT LAURA: I expect we have almost anything you need.

CRAWFISH CHARLIE: Well, my name is Crawfish Charlie, the cook of this here trail drive, and I need almost anything you have.

(Jake and Jenny rush behind counter and pile items into basket as he calls them out.)

CRAWFISH CHARLIE: Let's see now *(counts off on fingers)*…I'll need flour and cornmeal, and some sourdough for the biscuits…green coffee, salt and sugar…better give me a few slabs of bacon and salt pork, a little soda and calomel for the digestion, and don't forget those pinto beans.

JAKE: Anything else, Mister Crawfish?

CRAWFISH CHARLIE: A bag of onions, perchance? That's a good lad.

JENNY: What about extra tallow for candles?

RAMON DIEGO: He will use the tallow for shortening, not candles.

HARVEY CORYELL: But we don't really want to see what we are eating, anyway.

CRAWFISH CHARLIE: *(shakes spoon at Harvey and Ramon)* Why you flea-bitten wooly wolves! Cowboys are the biggest crybabies in the world!

RAMON DIEGO: He is right, you know. Here is a song from Mexico called *Soy Pobre Vaquero—I Am a Poor Cowboy.*

(Ramon stands next to Crawfish Charlie and sings to him. MUSIC: "Soy Pobre Vaquero.")

RAMON DIEGO: *(SINGS)*
    Soy pobre vaquero
    No tengo padre
    Ni hermana, ni hermano
RAMON DIEGO, HARVEY CORYELL, AUNT LAURA,
JAKE & JENNY: *(SING)*
    O no, O no, O no
RAMON DIEGO: *(SINGS)*
    Soy pobre vaquero
    No tengo madre
    Ni hermana, ni hermano
RAMON DIEGO, HARVEY CORYELL, AUNT LAURA,
JAKE & JENNY: *(SING)*
    O no, O no, O no
RAMON DIEGO: *(SINGS)*
    Soy pobre vaquero
    No tengo gato
    Ni perro, ni caballo
CRAWFISH CHARLIE: *(SINGS)*
    O no, O no, O no

(Ramon Diego and Harvey Coryell hoot and holler and clap Crawfish Charlie on the back.)

HARVEY CORYELL: Well, folks, I reckon it is time for us to hit the trail and start moving those dogies.
AUNT LAURA: Gentlemen, one favor before you go?
HARVEY CORYELL: Yes, ma'am?
AUNT LAURA: What exactly is a "dogie"?
HARVEY CORYELL: A "dogie" is a young steer, not yet a year old. It is too small for market and has to be fattened up before it can be sold. And when it walks beside its mother, it looks kinda like a little puppy dog.
RAMON DIEGO: Con permiso, amigo—"dogie" comes from the Spanish word *dogal*, which means "halter" or "noose," which is what the first cowboys, or *vaqueros*, used to lead the cattle.

CRAWFISH CHARLIE: Awww, you *lobos* are *loco!* Everybody knows the word "dogie" comes from "dough guts"—a calf that's so skinny, its belly looks like a sack of dough!

(All laugh and walk to center stage, where they are joined by Jesse Chisholm, Joseph McCoy, Army Officer, Railroad Engineer and the herd of longhorn Cattle entering from left. MUSIC: "Git Along, Little Dogies.")

HARVEY CORYELL: *(SINGS)*
　　As I was out walking one morning for pleasure
　　I spied a cowpuncher a-riding along
RAMON DIEGO: *(SINGS)*
　　His hat was throwed back and his spurs were a jingling
　　And as he advanced, he was singing this song
ALL: *(SING)*
　　Whoopee-ti-yi-yo, git along, little dogies
　　It's your misfortune and none of my own
　　Whoopee-ti-yi-yo, git along, little dogies
　　Abilene, Kansas will be your new home
JAKE: *(SINGS)*
　　It's early in spring that we round up the dogies
　　We mark them and brand them and bob off their tails
JENNY: *(SINGS)*
　　We round up our horses, load up the chuck wagon
　　And then throw the dogies out onto the trail
ALL: *(SING)*
　　Whoopee-ti-yi-yo, git along, little dogies
　　It's your misfortune and none of my own
　　Whoopee-ti-yi-yo, git along, little dogies
　　Abilene, Kansas will be your new home
　　Abilene, Kansas will be your new home
CATTLE: Moooooooooooo!

(LIGHTS OUT.)

* THE END *

Git Along, Little Dogies

(traditional, arranged by L.E. McCullough)

As I was out walk- ing one mor- ning for plea- sure, I spied a cow- pun-cher a- ri- ding a- long; His hat was throwed back and his spurs were a jing- ling and as he ad- vanced, he was sing- ing this song: Whoo-pee ti- yi- yo —— git a- long, lit-tle do- gies; it's your mis- for- tune and none of my own; Whoo-pee ti- yi- yo —— git a- long, lit- tle do- gies, A- bi- lene, Kan- sas will be your new home

Soy Pobre Vaquero

(traditional, arranged by L.E. McCullough)

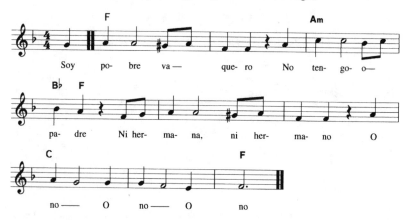

Soy po- bre va — que- ro   No ten- go- o—
pa- dre   Ni her- ma- na,   ni her- ma- no   O
no —— O   no —— O   no

§ English Translation §

Verse 1   I am a poor cowboy / I have no father / Nor sister nor brother / O no, O no, O no

Verse 2   I am a poor cowboy / I have no mother / Nor sister nor brother / O no, O no, O no

Verse 3   I am a poor cowboy / I have no cat / Nor dog nor horse / O no, O no, O no

The Old Chisholm Trail

(traditional, arranged by L.E. McCullough)

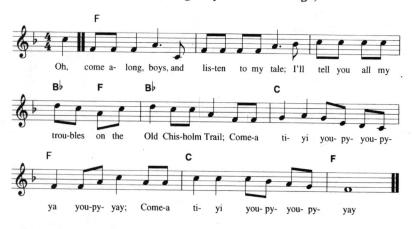

Oh, come a- long, boys, and lis- ten to my tale; I'll tell you all my
trou- bles on the Old Chis- holm Trail; Come-a ti- yi you- py- you- py-
ya you- py- yay; Come-a ti- yi you- py- you- py- yay

THE GOLDEN SPIKE

With the uniting of the East and West Coasts by one continuous railroad line in 1869, the United States became truly one nation, with goods and people able to move freely and comfortably throughout the land across the highest mountains, the driest deserts and widest rivers. Until then, it had taken five months to cross the continent by horse, wagon and steamboat; by train, a traveler could reach San Francisco from New York in a mere eight days. However, this tremendous feat was accomplished at an enormous cost in human lives—thousands of railroad workers died during the six years it took to build the 1,776 miles of Union Pacific and Central Pacific Railroad track, the final links in the chain of railroads spanning the U.S. The construction of the Western railroads also hastened the destruction of many Native American tribes whose hunting grounds were sold off to tens of thousands of ranchers and homesteaders arriving by train.

TIME: May 10, 1869

PLACE: Promontory Point, Utah

CAST: 30 actors, min. 11 boys, 2 girls

Anna Pierce Judah	Theodore Judah
Thomas Durant	Leland Stanford
Charles Crocker	Collis Huntington
Mark Hopkins	Telegraph Operator
Photographer	Tribune Reporter
Herald Reporter	Congressman
Jack Casement	Dan Casement
6 Union Pacific Tracklayers	Jane Pierce
6 Central Pacific Tracklayers	James Strobridge
Mr. Coe	Jared Pierce

RUNNING TIME: 20 minutes

STAGE SET: railroad tie with golden spike, rocking chair, two ties, a rail

PROPS: telegraph key, camera and tripod, 2 pencils, 2 notebooks, silver sledge with a wire attached to telegraph key, newspaper, 2 hand-held American flags, survey papers

EFFECTS: Visual—lights flash for camera flash; Sound—sledge hammer clanging on rail

MUSIC: *Working on the Railway*.

COSTUMES: All characters dress in period costumes befitting occupation and status; Central Pacific Tracklayers should dress as 1860s Chinese workers—loose-fitting blue tunics and pantaloons with inverted basket-shaped straw hats

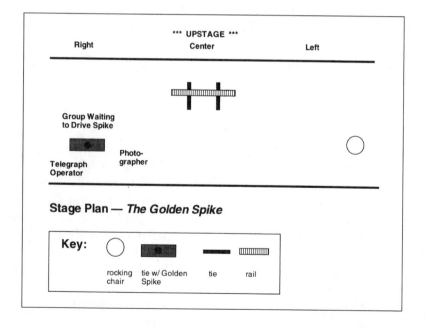

(LIGHTS UP RIGHT on a crowd gathered down right around the Golden Spike: Thomas Durant and Leland Stanford ringed by Three Union Pacific Tracklayers and Three Central Pacific Tracklayers. To their right a Telegraph Operator squats at his telegraph key; to their left a Photographer hunches over his camera and tripod aimed to take their picture; at center stage Two Newspaper Reporters stand, scribbling in their notebooks.)

TRIBUNE REPORTER: Chicago Tribune, May 10, 1869, two-forty-two p.m., Eastern time. Here at Promontory Point, Utah—in a stark desert landscape filled with only scrub, sagebrush and the occasional startled jackrabbit—a crowd has gathered to mark a momentous event in human history...the completion of the first continuous railroad line across North America!

PHOTOGRAPHER: *(to the group, motioning)* Say, there, fella, could you move to the left a little? Don't crowd, don't crowd now!

HERALD REPORTER: New York Herald, Five-Star Extra! Colonel Charles Savage, the renowned Salt Lake City photographer, has been engaged to record the exact moment when Thomas Durant, President of the Union Pacific Railroad, and California Governor Leland Crocker of the Central Pacific Railroad, drive in the final spike that will unite the Atlantic and Pacific oceans with one long iron rail!

TELEGRAPH OPERATOR: *(looks around, peers out into audience)* Where's the fella with the gumdiddled sledge?

(Group shrugs their shoulders.)

TELEGRAPH OPERATOR: I said, where's the fella with the gumdiddled sledge?

TRIBUNE REPORTER: The final spike—a bright golden spike—will be driven into the railroad tie by a silver sledge.

HERALD REPORTER: Attached to the sledge is a wire connected to the telegraph key. When the sledge hits the spike—

TRIBUNE REPORTER: Western Union telegraph operator W.N. Shilling will transmit the signal to the entire nation! Three quick taps signaling "Done"!

TELEGRAPH OPERATOR: For crying out loud, where's the fella—

(Mr. Coe enters from right with the silver sledge and hands it to Leland Stanford.)

MR. COE: *(tips hat in apology)* Sorry, gentlemen. *(takes his place at rear of group)*

HERALD REPORTER: Mr. Coe, representing the Pacific Union Express, hands the silver sledge to Governor Stanford.

TRIBUNE REPORTER: The band stops playing...

HERALD REPORTER: A hush falls over the assembly...

TRIBUNE REPORTER: Governor Stanford hoists the sledge...

HERALD REPORTER: All America awaits the mighty blow...

(All characters freeze; LIGHTS OUT. The Three Union Pacific Tracklayers and Three Central Pacific Tracklayers offstage sing as characters in first scene exit right. MUSIC: "Working on the Railway.")

TRACKLAYERS: *(SING, O.S.)*
In eighteen hundred and forty-one
I put my corduroy britches on
Then my time had just begun
Working on the railway

Fiddle-ee-or-ee-or-ee-ay
Fiddle-ee-or-ee-or-ee-i;
Fiddle-ee-or-ee-or-ee-ay
Working on the railway

(LIGHTS UP LEFT on Anna Pierce Judah, sitting in a rocking chair at down left reading a newspaper; her niece and nephew, Jane and Jared Pierce, dash in from left waving American flags.)

JANE PIERCE: Aunt Anna! Come with us downtown!

JARED PIERCE: There is a parade on Main Street for the railroad!

JANE PIERCE: A brass band is playing!

JARED PIERCE: All the churches are going to ring their bells when they drive the Golden Spike!

JANE PIERCE: It is the most exciting day that ever happened in Greenfield, Massachusetts!

JARED PIERCE: Or anywhere! Come with us to the parade, Aunt Anna! Please?

ANNA JUDAH PIERCE: No, children, I am too old for parades. But you are right about this day, May 10, being a most exciting day. I see the papers are calling it "the Wedding of the Rails." *(chuckles)* Well, twenty-two years ago this day there was another wedding...your uncle Theodore and I were married.

(LIGHTS UP CENTER on Theodore Judah standing at down center with survey papers in his hand, facing audience; LIGHTS FADE OUT LEFT.)

ANNA JUDAH PIERCE: Theodore had loved railroads ever since he was a boy. When he was only thirteen, he had worked on the Schenectady and Troy Railroad as a surveyor's assistant. He was an associate engineer on the Erie Canal, and then built railroads throughout New York and New England. In 1854 we went to California, and he built the Sacramento Valley Railroad, the first railroad west of the Mississippi.

(Theodore Judah begins pacing at center, alternately studying his papers and shaking them in his fists. Charles Crocker enters from left, Collis Huntington and Mark Hopkins enter from right and walk briskly across stage; they are hailed by Theodore Judah and stop and listen to him.)

ANNA JUDAH PIERCE: *(O.S.)* But that was not enough for Theodore. Like many others, he dreamed of a railroad that would span the continent. We spent the next few years surveying and mapping out a route over the Sierra Nevada Mountains, and Theodore shared his vision with anyone who would listen.

THEODORE JUDAH: The men who build a railroad across this land will be the kings of the age!

ANNA JUDAH PIERCE: *(O.S.)* In 1861, Theodore and a group of Sacramento businessmen founded the Central Pacific Railroad Company and raised a small amount of money. The Company sent him to Washington, D.C. to ask the Federal Government to grant land and treasury bonds.

(Crocker, Huntington and Hopkins shake hands with Theodore Judah and exit left; Congressman enters from right and is approached by Theodore Judah.)

ANNA JUDAH PIERCE: *(O.S.)* It was the third time Theodore had gone to Washington to speak for the railroad, and this time he succeeded.

CONGRESSMAN: *(to audience)* July 1, 1862, President Abraham Lincoln signs the Pacific Railroad Act. The Central Pacific will start from Sacramento and build east; the Union Pacific will begin at Omaha and build west. The railroads will meet at Salt Lake City, Utah Territory. Each company will receive sixteen thousand dollars per mile of track laid in the lowlands, forty-eight thousand dollars for each mile laid in the mountains.

THEODORE JUDAH: We have drawn the elephant. Now let us see if we can harness him up. *(shakes hands with Congressman, exits left; Congressman exits right. LIGHTS OUT CENTER.)*

ANNA JUDAH PIERCE: *(O.S.)* But poor Theodore would never see his dream become a reality. While crossing the Isthmus of Panama, he caught yellow fever...and died...November 2, 1863.

(Three Union Pacific Tracklayers and Three Central Pacific Tracklayers offstage sing. MUSIC: "Working on the Railway.")

TRACKLAYERS: *(SING, O.S.)*
    In eighteen hundred and sixty-three
    I sailed away across the sea
    I sailed to Californi-ay
    Working on the railway

    Fiddle-ee-or-ee-or-ee-ay
    Fiddle-ee-or-ee-or-ee-i;
    Fiddle-ee-or-ee-or-ee-ay
    Working on the railway

(LIGHTS UP CENTER on Jack and Dan Casement standing at down center.)

ANNA JUDAH PIERCE: *(O.S.)* Not much work could be done until the Civil War ended in 1865. Then the building began in earnest, an army of workers swarming over the plains and deserts.

JACK CASEMENT: *(to audience)* My name is General Jack Casement, this is my brother Dan. We are the crew leaders of the Union Pacific. You'll work hard for us, but you'll be well-paid—two dollars a day.

DAN CASEMENT: An extra dollar if you lay more than a mile of track.

JACK CASEMENT: Every man has a job—the same job—every hour, every day. Your day begins at dawn with breakfast: beef, beans, potatoes, fresh bread and plenty of strong coffee or tea. We know you lads from Ireland will appreciate the spuds and tea.

UNION PACIFIC TRACKLAYERS: *(O.S.)* Hurrah, hurrah for Erin go bragh!

DAN CASEMENT: Then the iron car pulls in and the hardware is unloaded. First, the ties are placed.

(Union Pacific Tracklayers #1 and #2 enter from left, each carrying a railroad tie they lay down at mid center stage.)

JACK CASEMENT: Then the rails are laid over the ties.

(Union Pacific Tracklayers #3 and #4 enter from left, carrying a long rail they lay over the ties as Tracklayers #1 and #2 exit right.)

DAN CASEMENT: And the spikes are driven into the rails.

(Union Pacific Tracklayers #5 and #6 enter from left and mime pounding spikes into the rail with a sledgehammer as Tracklayers #3 and #4 exit right; after a few strokes, Tracklayers #5 and #6 exit right.)

JACK CASEMENT: And the whole cycle starts over again, moving forward as fast as a man can walk.

DAN CASEMENT: Stopping for nothing—

JACK CASEMENT: Not Indian raids—

DAN CASEMENT : Not disease and illness—

JACK CASEMENT: Not injuries or brawls—

DAN CASEMENT: Not buffalo stampedes or snowstorms—

JACK CASEMENT: Nothing to stop the fiery iron tide flowing across the land.

(LIGHTS OUT CENTER as Six Union Pacific Tracklayers off-stage sing. MUSIC: "Working on the Railway.")

TRACKLAYERS: (SING, O.S.)
In eighteen hundred and sixty-five
I felt myself but half-alive
I came upon the Western drive
Working on the railway

Fiddle-ee-or-ee-or-ee-ay
Fiddle-ee-or-ee-or-ee-i;
Fiddle-ee-or-ee-or-ee-ay
Working on the railway

(LIGHTS UP CENTER on Charles Crocker and James Strobridge standing at down center, facing each other.)

ANNA JUDAH PIERCE: (O.S.) But in California, it was tough going for the Central Pacific. By 1865, only thirty-one miles of track had been completed. Many of the workers ran off to the silver fields of Nevada or simply quit when the railroad became bogged down in the mountains. Finally, the railroad's construction chief, Charles Crocker, told his chief engineer, James Strobridge, to take drastic action.

CHARLES CROCKER: Strobridge, we can't find enough qualified workers. I want you to go to Sacramento and hire fifty Chinese to work on the railroad.

JAMES STROBRIDGE: Hire Chinese? Crocker, you must be mad! The average Chinaman weighs a hundred pounds. They're a bunch of rice-eating weaklings! How can they build a railroad?

CHARLES CROCKER: They built the Great Wall of China, didn't they? Hire them! Now!

(James Strobridge exits left; Six Central Pacific Tracklayers enter from left and busily mime track laying and spike driving motions on rails at mid center.)

CHARLES CROCKER: The public was outraged. How dare the Central Pacific take jobs away from Americans! By the end of 1865 seven thousand Chinese were at work on the Central Pacific, and work was going faster than ever. In fact, because of the Chinese working so quickly, we were able to hire more Americans. We kept the peace with the Shoshone and Paiute Indians, too, by hiring them—and their squaws—to work alongside the Chinese. During 1868, we laid a mile of track every day! It looked like the Central Pacific would win the race to Salt Lake City!

(LIGHTS OUT CENTER as Six Union Pacific Tracklayers offstage sing. MUSIC: "Working on the Railway.")

TRACKLAYERS: *(SING, O.S.)*
  In eighteen hundred and sixty-eight
  We drove across the desert straight
  We didn't even hesitate
  Working on the railway

  Fiddle-ee-or-ee-or-ee-ay
  Fiddle-ee-or-ee-or-ee-i;
  Fiddle-ee-or-ee-or-ee-ay
  Working on the railway

(LIGHTS UP CENTER on Leland Stanford, Thomas Durant and the Congressman standing at down center, facing audience.)

ANNA JUDAH PIERCE: *(O.S.)* Early in 1869, the Central Pacific and Union Pacific crews caught sight of each other in northern Nevada, just a stone's throw apart. Instead of stopping, however, each company kept on laying track past the other. What nonsense! I know my Theodore wouldn't have stood for it.

CONGRESSMAN: Governor Stanford, Dr. Durant—this is an outrage! Your ridiculous competition is costing the taxpayers millions of dollars!

LELAND STANFORD: By the terms of the original agreement, we are being paid for every mile of track we lay. We have a right to earn money to pay back our investors.

CONGRESSMAN: But you are supposed to meet up in Salt Lake City!

THOMAS DURANT: We will...but the agreement doesn't say when...or how many miles it takes for us to get there.

CONGRESSMAN: I spoke with President Grant this morning, and he is most concerned. He said, and I quote, "If Durant and Stanford cannot choose a meeting place for their railroads, I will choose one."

LELAND STANFORD: That sounds rather final, wouldn't you say, Dr. Durant?

THOMAS DURANT: It does, indeed, Governor.

CONGRESSMAN: Very well, I will notify the President. Good day. *(exits right)*

LELAND STANFORD: Well, that's all settled. I'll see you in Utah. *(turns to exit right)*

THOMAS DURANT: One moment, Governor. We still have one unfinished piece of business. Last fall Charles Crocker boasted his Central Pacific crews could lay down ten miles of track in one day.

LELAND STANFORD: And you don't believe him?

THOMAS DURANT: Let's just say I'm extremely skeptical. Would you wish to back him up by means of a small wager?

LELAND STANFORD: I'll back him to the tune of ten thousand dollars, Doctor. A thousand dollars for every mile!

(Stanford and Durant shake hands and exit right; Six Central Pacific Tracklayers and Charles Crocker enter from left and cross to mid center. The Tracklayers are hunched over the rails, Charles Crocker stands to their left with his arm raised.)

ANNA JUDAH PIERCE: *(O.S.)* At seven o'clock on the morning of April 28, 1869, on a flat grade just west of Blue Creek, Utah, Charles Crocker gave the signal.

CHARLES CROCKER: *(lowers his arm)* You're off!

(The tracklayers begin work motions, miming laying ties, setting rails and driving spikes.)

ANNA JUDAH PIERCE: *(O.S.)* It was, one witness said, a feat that rivaled the labors of Hercules. By half-past one in the afternoon, the crew had reached the six-mile mark. When they finished at seven that night, ten miles and fifty-six feet of track had been laid using 25,800 ties, 3,520 rails, 28,160 spikes— 144 feet of track a minute.

(LIGHTS OUT CENTER, LIGHTS UP RIGHT. Stanford and Durant are back at right among group gathered around the Golden Spike; Stanford holds the silver sledge over his head.)

TRIBUNE REPORTER: Governor Stanford hoists the sledge...
HERALD REPORTER: All America awaits the mighty blow...

(Stanford brings down the sledge but misses the Golden Spike; Tracklayers howl.)

TRIBUNE REPORTER: He missed! He missed the Golden Spike!

(Stanford hands sledge to Durant, who hoists it aloft.)

HERALD REPORTER: And now Thomas Durant takes the sledge...

(Durant brings down the sledge and misses the Golden Spike; Tracklayers howl.)

TRIBUNE REPORTER: And Durant misses the Spike!
TELEGRAPH REPORTER: Oh, the heck with it! *(taps telegraph key three times)* Done!

(Tracklayers grapple for sledge.)

TRACKLAYERS: The Golden Spike! It's mine! I'll do it! Give it here!
PHOTOGRAPHER: Everybody, smile!

(Tracklayers stop, everyone freezes, Photographer clicks camera. VISUAL EFFECT: LIGHTS FLASH. LIGHTS OUT RIGHT. LIGHTS UP LEFT.)

JARED PIERCE: That sure is an exciting tale, Aunt Anna. Too bad Uncle Theodore couldn't be at Promontory Point today to see his dream come true.

JANE PIERCE: Aunt Anna, do you wish you could have been there?

ANNA PIERCE JUDAH: Maybe it is the sweet spring air. Or the birds trilling their songs of beauty above. But in some special way, children, I believe the spirit of my brave husband has descended upon me, and together we *are* there.

(SOUND: sledge hammer clanging on rail. MUSIC: "Working on the Railway.")

TRACKLAYERS: *(SING)*
In eighteen hundred and sixty-nine
I thought myself so very fine
How that Golden Spike did shine
Working on the railway

ALL CAST: *(SING)*
Fiddle-ee-or-ee-or-ee-ay
Fiddle-ee-or-ee-or-ee-i;
Fiddle-ee-or-ee-or-ee-ay
Working on the railway

Fiddle-ee-or-ee-or-ee-ay
Fiddle-ee-or-ee-or-ee-i;
Fiddle-ee-or-ee-or-ee-ay
Working on the railway

(LIGHTS OUT.)

* THE END *

Working on the Railway
(traditional, arranged by L.E. McCullough)

In eigh- teen hun- dred and for- ty- one I
put my cor- du- roy brit- ches on; Then my time had
just be- gun work- ing on the rail- way Fid- dle- ee- or- ee-
or- ee- ay! Fid- dle- ee- or- ee- or- ee- i!
Fid- dle- ee- or- ee- or- ee- ay! Work- ing on the rail- way!

GREAT MEDICINE PAINTER

George Catlin (1796–1872) was the first American artist to venture into the West for the specific purpose of recording the life and culture of the Native American tribes. He spent years painting chiefs and warriors, medicine men and squaws, children at play. He also collected the tribes' material culture: weapons, costumes, ritual items, tools and household goods. During a time when most Americans back East thought Indians were simple savages, Catlin's paintings and books helped show that the Indians possessed a complex and sophisticated culture deserving of respect and preservation. After his death, Catlin's artwork was given to the Smithsonian Institution in Washington, D.C. and the American Museum of National History in New York.

TIME: 1830s

PLACE: Where the buffalo once roamed

CAST: 17 actors, min. 7 boys, 5 girls

George Catlin	Chouteau
One Horn	Little Horse
Short Bull	2 Sioux Women
2 Sioux Men	Ticket Seller
2 Art Critics	Congressman
Mrs. McCracken	Donna
Daryl	Debbi

RUNNING TIME: 20 minutes

STAGE SET: 4 desks, 4 chairs, flatboat rudder, 2 stools, easel

PROPS: ruler, 2 books, Donna's sketchpad and pencil, George Catlin's sketchpad and pencil, portrait of One Horn, paint brush

MUSIC: *Shenandoah, Song of the Spirit Dance*

COSTUMES: Characters dress as befitting their time period, occupation and social status; George Catlin as depicted in 1849 portrait by William Fisk—light brown fringed buckskin tunic and buckskin pants, a brown leather belt, fringed leather boots

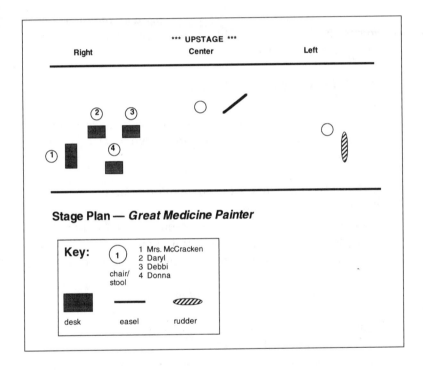

Stage Plan — *Great Medicine Painter*

(LIGHTS UP RIGHT on a classroom at down right. Mrs. McCracken sits at her desk monitoring a study session—Donna, Daryl and Debbi are at desks, Daryl playing with a ruler, Debbi ostensibly reading but actually watching Donna, who is drawing intently on a sketchpad.)

MRS. MCCRACKEN: I will have your mathematics quiz graded by tomorrow, children. You may spend the next ten minutes studying on your own—*quietly. (begins reading from book)*
DONNA: Yes, Mrs. McCracken.

(Bored, Daryl becomes increasingly silly with the ruler; Debbi looks over Donna's shoulder and nudges Daryl to look at Donna's drawing.)

DARYL: *(whispering to Debbi)* Look at me, I'm a spaceman!

(He giggles, puts ruler atop his head; Debbi giggles, coughs, chokes, sputters in effort to restrain giggling; Donna continues to draw.)

MRS. MCCRACKEN: What is the commotion? Daryl?
DARYL: *(raises hand)* Present!
MRS. MCCRACKEN: I *know* you're present, Daryl. I want to know *why* you're disrupting the class study time.
DARYL: Ummmmm…take me to your leader! *(salutes with ruler)*

(Debbi breaks out in a sputter of giggling.)

MRS. MCCRACKEN: That's enough! Debbi, Daryl, would you care to visit the principal's office?
DEBBI: *(stands)* I'm sorry, Mrs. McCracken. It's just that Donna is drawing funny pictures again. *(sits)*
MRS. MCCRACKEN: Donna.
(Donna continues to draw.)
MRS. MCCRACKEN: Donna!
DONNA: *(startled, looks up)* Eight times seven equals fifty-six!
MRS. MCCRACKEN: Donna, show me what you're drawing.

(Donna rises, lays sketchpad on desk; Mrs. McCracken turns the pages.)

MRS. MCCRACKEN: Donna, what are these...things?
DONNA: They're people that live on other planets.

(Debbi and Daryl burst out giggling.)

MRS. MCCRACKEN: Silence!

(Debbi and Daryl quiet.)

MRS. MCCRACKEN: These are very detailed, Donna. You have quite a vivid imagination.
DONNA: Thank you, Mrs. McCracken. Of course, I've never been to another planet. But I did see some moon rocks when our family visited the NASA museum in Houston last summer. And that got me thinking: someday people from Earth will travel to other planets and meet other creatures. What will they look like?
DARYL: Duh, like aliens, maybe?
DONNA: How will they dress?
DEBBI: Space Gap for Space Kids!
DONNA: What customs will they have?
DARYL: Brushing their teeth with their elbow? *(mimes)*
MRS. MCCRACKEN: *(hands sketchpad to Donna)* You know, class, it may seem like Donna is wasting her time drawing things we've never seen, but she's actually in very good company. In the early 1800s most Americans lived East of the Mississippi. And they had never seen any of the Native American tribes who lived west of the Mississippi. Nor did they know what buffalo looked like. Or the Rocky Mountains or Pike's Peak. People thought about the West then the way we think about outer space today—something very alien and far away.
DEBBI: Couldn't they take pictures?
MRS. MCCRACKEN: The camera wasn't invented until 1839 and wasn't very portable until the 1850s.

DARYL: Hadn't the Lewis and Clark Expedition already explored the West?

MRS. MCCRACKEN: Yes, they had, Daryl, but they only saw a very small part. And no one had taken the time to systematically record what was really out in the great plains and deserts, until the painter George Catlin left St. Louis on a flatboat in the fall of 1830, headed up the Missouri River with a band of fur trappers.

(LIGHTS OUT RIGHT; LIGHTS UP LEFT on George Catlin and the flatboat helmsman, Chouteau, at down left. Chouteau steers the rudder and stares out at the audience while Catlin sits on the stool and sketches Chouteau. MUSIC: "Shenandoah" sung by offstage chorus as lighting changes.)

CHORUS: *(SING, O.S.)*
O, Shenandoah, I long to hear you
Away you rolling river
O, Shenandoah, I long to hear you
Away, I'm bound away
Across the wide Missouri

GEORGE CATLIN: Have you been trapping in the West long, Monsieur Chouteau?

CHOUTEAU: Most longer than you've been alive, I reckon. What's an educated Eastern dandy like you doing headed out to the Great American Desert?

GEORGE CATLIN: I was a lawyer in Pennsylvania for some years. I increasingly found myself at trial making idle sketches of the defendant, the witnesses, even the judge and jury. Anything to take my mind off the boredom of the court! I decided I would be of greater service painting people than defending them.

CHOUTEAU: There's blamed few people to paint out this way.

GEORGE CATLIN: On the contrary! The land is filled with Indians! My goal is to reach every tribe on the continent and bring home faithful portraits of their principal personages. Along with full notes of their character and history for the use and instruction of future ages.

CHOUTEAU: You've come to paint Indians, eh? Don't know why you bother. As the white man moves west and brings his farms and his factories, the Indians will disappear like dust in the wind. There won't even *be* any Indians in twenty years.

GEORGE CATLIN: Maybe so, monsieur. And that is why I must paint them now.

(LIGHTS OUT LEFT.)

MRS. MCCRACKEN: *(O.S.)* Catlin visited many tribes on that first trip upriver—the Iowa, Delaware and Potawatomie...the Sac, Kickapoo and Peoria...the Kaskaskia, Omaha and Fox. He even painted the Shawnee Prophet, the brother of the great Eastern warrior Tecumseh, who had nearly succeeded in driving the Americans out of Indiana and Illinois just twenty years before.

(MUSIC: "Song of the Spirit Dance" sung by offstage chorus as LIGHTS UP CENTER on One Horn, Little Horse and George Catlin at mid center. One Horn sits on stool facing audience as Catlin stands at the easel to his left, painting the Sioux chief's portrait; the interpreter, Little Horse, stands to the right of One Horn.)

CHORUS: *(SING, O.S.)*
  Ya ha e hi ya
  Ya ha e hi ya
  He ya e yo e yo e-e-e

MRS. MCCRACKEN: *(O.S.)* Two years later, in May, 1832, Catlin was at Fort Pierre, visiting the Sioux—the greatest warrior tribe of the Western Plains. Like most of the Indians Catlin met, the Sioux had never seen a life-like portrait of themselves. And so, the first painting he was allowed to make was a portrait of One Horn, the main Sioux chief. A lesser Sioux chief, Little Horse, translated between the painter and his subject.

LITTLE HORSE: One Horn is big chief of Sioux. Very brave. Has many scalps. One Horn can outrun buffalo, outrun arrows, outrun lightning and thunder.

GEORGE CATLIN: Tell One Horn I am honored to be in the presence of such a strong warrior. His power gives my painting good medicine.

(The medicine man Short Bull enters from left, followed by Two Sioux Men and Two Sioux Women; they cross to center and stare at the portrait, murmuring as Catlin pauses.)

LITTLE HORSE: This is Short Bull, medicine man. He means big trouble.

(Short Bull and the Sioux Men and Women begin shouting and stomping in anger, circling around the easel; Short Bull tries to grab portrait from easel but Catlin holds him back; One Horn leaps off stool and stops all action by thrusting his arms outward.)

SHORT BULL: One Horn, you are a fool! Your spirit has been stolen and trapped in this paper! *(points to portrait)* Look, your eyes are open—you will never be able to sleep!

(Sioux Men and Women wail.)

ONE HORN: Cease your wailing! *(picks up paint brush)* This is hair of horse. *(points to portrait)* This is water and sand and clay. These things may frighten Short Bull...they do not frighten One Horn.

SHORT BULL: Beware, mighty chief. Those painted with magic brushes will soon die. These pictures have captured life—your life—which now lives in enemies' hands. After you die, your soul will wander the earth as a ghost!

GEORGE CATLIN: *(to One Horn)* Short Bull has powerful medicine. And he is right that my magic brushes have powerful medicine, too. *(holds portrait)* I have brought this medicine a long distance—to paint pictures of the great Sioux chiefs and to show them to the great white chiefs. When the white chiefs see pictures of the Sioux, they will know the Sioux as strong warriors and will know they must honor them.

LITTLE HORSE: What say you, One Horn?

ONE HORN: This Medicine Painter was made as the Great Spirit created him. He was made to paint all the tribes with brushes and with words. His medicine is good. It is for the good of our people a long time from now, good for others in the world to see who we are. The white man does not want to listen to the Indian. These pictures will speak for us.

(MUSIC: "Song of the Spirit Dance" sung by offstage chorus as One Horn, Little Horse, Short Bull and the Sioux Men and Women dance in a circle then single file as they exit left.)

CHORUS: *(SING, O.S.)*
   Ya ha e hi ya
   Ya ha e hi ya
   He ya e yo e yo e-e-e

   Ya ha e hi ya
   Ya ha e hi ya
   He ya e yo e yo e-e-e

(LIGHTS OUT CENTER.)

MRS. MCCRACKEN: *(O.S.)* George Catlin was determined that Americans back East understand and appreciate the culture of the American Indian. In 1837, after he had painted forty-eight tribes in travels extending as far south as Texas and as far west as Wyoming, he came to New York City and opened an exhibit on Broadway.

(LIGHTS UP LEFT on a Ticket Seller at down left, hawking tickets.)

TICKET SELLER: Get your tickets to the wonder of the age— Catlin's Indian Gallery! Only fifty cents, ladies and gentlemen, half-price for children—three hundred and thirty portraits of the most distinguished members of those uncivilized regions! Together with a large collection of gen-u-wine bows, quivers, spears, shields, moccasins, belts, pouches, clubs, wampum, whistles, rattles and drums!

(Two Art Critics enter from left and buy tickets.)

TICKET SELLER: You're quite lucky, gentlemen, it's been standing room only for weeks!

(Ticket Seller exits left; Art Critics move to mid center and stroll about as if looking at pictures.)

ART CRITIC #1: Truly one of the most remarkable and interesting works the genius and labor of an individual has created in this age and country!

ART CRITIC #2: Uncouth rubbish!

(Congressman and George Catlin enter from left and listen to Art Critics.)

ART CRITIC #1: One of the most striking triumphs the pencil has ever achieved!

ART CRITIC #2: Childish poppycock!

(Art Critics stop at down center, facing audience; Art Critic #1 turns menacingly to Art Critic #2.)

ART CRITIC #1: Mr. Catlin has accomplished a work that will forever associate his name in the highest rank of honor!

ART CRITIC #2: *(in Art Critic #1's face)* Mr. Catlin couldn't draw a buffalo with both hands in broad daylight!

(Art Critics stroll offstage right, exit.)

CONGRESSMAN: I see your exhibit stirs deep emotions.

GEORGE CATLIN: It is intended to, Congressman. After all the abuse suffered from invasion, fraud and deception, the Indian in his native state remains honest and hospitable. They are a people who have always made me welcome to the best they had...a people who are honest without laws, who have no jails and no poorhouse...who never take the name of God in vain...who never fought a battle with white men except on their own ground...and, oh, how I love a people who don't live for the love of money!

CONGRESSMAN: Those are very strong sentiments, sir. I'm not certain how the rest of Congress will cotton to them. America is, as you know, advancing westward by leaps and bounds. Nothing—or no one—can stand in the way.

GEORGE CATLIN: Indeed, sir, nothing—short of the loss of my own life—can stand in the way of my pleading the case of our country's native tribes. I pledge my word—and my life—to that solemn purpose.

(LIGHTS OUT CENTER; LIGHTS UP RIGHT on classroom.)

DARYL: Gosh, Mrs. McCracken, that sure was interesting. I always thought Peoria and Omaha were just names of cities.

MRS. MCCRACKEN: They were named for Native American tribes, tribes that have long vanished and are remembered only in the paintings of George Catlin and other artists of the early 1800s. George Catlin left us the only permanent record of how these Indians lived—or that they had ever lived at all. He showed us an entire unknown world.

DEBBI: Did George Catlin go on to paint more American Indians?

MRS. MCCRACKEN: George Catlin was very outspoken about the bad ways the American government treated the Indians. Because of this, he became unpopular here and spent most of the rest of his life in Europe and South America, where he spent five years painting dozens of native tribes. He was also the first person to suggest a national park system for the United States—and a national museum. After he died in 1872 at age 77, his collection of paintings and Native American artifacts was given to the Smithsonian Institution, where it is on exhibit today. So you see, children, Donna may be drawing what we think is a strange world, but someday we'll need an artist of her talents to record what lies beyond our reach.

DARYL: Gee, Donna, I'm sorry I laughed at your weird drawings. They're really pretty neat.

DEBBI: Maybe by the time we grow up, we *will* find creatures on other planets. And you'll be there to show us what they look like!

DONNA: Maybe. I just hope we get along better with aliens than we did our Native Americans.

(MUSIC: "Shenandoah" sung by offstage chorus as LIGHTS

FADE OUT; after verse of "Shenandoah," MUSIC segues into "Song of the Spirit Dance" sung by offstage chorus.)

CHORUS: *(SING, O.S.)*

O, Shenandoah, I long to hear you
Away you rolling river
O, Shenandoah, I long to hear you
Away, I'm bound away
Across the wide Missouri

Ya ha e hi ya
Ya ha e hi ya
He ya e yo e yo e-e-e

Ya ha e hi ya
Ya ha e hi ya
He ya e yo e yo e-e-e

* THE END *

Shenandoah

(traditional, arranged by L.E. McCullough)

O, Shen- an- doah, I long to hear you! A-—— way you roll- ing ri- ver! O, Shen- an- doah, I long to hear you! A-— way, I'm bound a- way! A-—— cross the wide Miss- ou- ri!

Song of the Spirit Dance

(traditional, arranged by L.E. McCullough)

Ya ha —— e hi —— ya Ya ha —— e hi —— ya He ya e —— yo e —— yo e- e- e

KLONDIKE FEVER

After the United States purchased Alaska from Russia in 1867, prospectors in search of gold began trickling into the frozen northern forests above the 49th parallel. The trickle turned into a flood in 1896 when the first big gold strike was found at Bonanza Creek between the Klondike and Yukon Rivers in Canada. One newcomer was Nellie Cashman (1851–1925), a native of Cork, Ireland, who had come to the United States in 1869 with her mother and sister. Nellie lived throughout the West prospecting and establishing boarding homes, restaurants and stores for miners. She hit paydirt several times but always gave her money away to those less fortunate; so renowned was Nellie for her charity and good deeds, that she became known as "the Miner's Angel," "the Angel of Tombstone" and "the Saint of the Sourdoughs." She settled in Dawson in 1898 and staked a claim on a gold mine near Bonanza Creek, earning over $100,000. In 1924, at age 73, she won the title of champion woman musher of Alaska, driving a dog-sled team 750 miles in 17 days. The Ingaliks are one of many Native American tribes who inhabited Alaska and northwestern Canada for centuries before the arrival of Europeans. A "cheechako" is a Klondike term meaning an inexperienced prospector or tenderfoot.

TIME: December, 1898—the Klondike Gold Rush

PLACE: Dawson, Yukon Territory, Canada

CAST: 14 actors, min. 5 boys, 1 girl

Sourdough Sam	Snowball (a Siberian Husky)
Nellie Cashman	Pig-Ear Pete
Cannibal Ike	Backstab Bill
2 Ingaliks	6 Polar Bears

RUNNING TIME: 20 minutes

STAGE SET: a table, a rock, a scrim depicting a tree-filled Alaskan mountainside, a standup sign reading "Moon Creek Mine"

PROPS: rolling pin, bread dough, map, 2 fishing poles, picnic basket, 6 gold nuggets, glove, pistol

COSTUMES: Sourdough Sam, Pig-Ear Pete, Backstab Bill and Cannibal Ike dress in late-19th century prospector duds; Nellie Cashman wears a nice late-19th century dress, perhaps with a bonnet; Ingaliks dress like prospectors but with some Native American accessories—feathers or headband or fringe; Snowball is costumed as a Siberian Husky and walks on all fours; Polar Bears wear white coverings and bodysuits so that when they are bent over on ground, they look like snow mounds

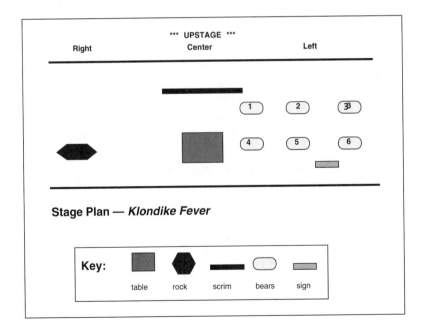

Stage Plan — *Klondike Fever*

Key: table rock scrim bears sign

(LIGHTS UP LEFT on Sourdough Sam, who stands at down left and addresses audience.)

SOURDOUGH SAM:
Hello, friends, come sit a spell
Just make yourselves at home.
Sourdough Sam is the name I tote
From Kodiak to Nome.
　I'll tell a tale of adventure true
To thrill both young and old,
A ripping yarn from the Klondike fields
That'll make your blood run cold.
　Twas in the Yukon up Dawson way
In eighteen and ninety-eight.
Gold was found and men went wild
Trying to win their stake.
　Thousands came from around the globe
Lured by a nugget's twinkling gleam,
Only to fail in the frozen ice
As they yielded up their dream.
　But some lucky few hit paydirt
In that land of the Midnight Sun.
Why, there's Miss Nellie Cashman
Whose story we've just begun!

(LIGHTS UP CENTER on Nellie Cashman standing to the right of a table, rolling bread dough with a rolling pin; her dog, Snowball, lies on the floor to the table's left; Nellie addresses audience.)

NELLIE:
He's right, my name it is Nellie;
From the shores of Ireland I came.
Following the trail of precious gems
Has been my lifelong aim.
　I've struck it rich a dozen times
In Tombstone and Cripple Creek.
Wherever the gold and silver flows
I extend my lucky streak.

But money to me means nothing;
Vast fortunes I've given away
To the poor, sick, unlucky miners
Cruel fate's seen fit to betray.
  They call me the "Miner's Angel"
Sometimes the "Sourdough Saint."
And about my homestyle cooking
You'll not hear one complaint!
  Now I run this jolly boarding house,
"Prospector's Haven" is the name.
Take a seat, if you will, and have some tea;
Mind the pup—don't fret, he's tame

(Snowball rises to his knees and addresses audience.)

SNOWBALL:

  Woof! Woof! I'm a dog and proud of it,
  The fierce blood of wolves heats my veins.
  But I allow my mistress to spoil me
  With spaghetti and chicken chow mein.

(Nellie holds up a piece of dough and incites Snowball to beg.)

NELLIE:

  Good doggie! Good Snowball! Snowball want a cookie?

(Snowball looks at Nellie, then back at audience, sorrowfully.)

SNOWBALL:

  It's a dog's life! Woof! *(begs, barks and catches treat, scuffling with it before finally eating it)*

NELLIE:

  Good doggie! *(returns to rolling dough)*

SNOWBALL:

  Well, it's true what she said about helping;
  She's saved many a poor starving man.
  But some folks think charity is weakness
  And take advantage however they can.

(Pig-Ear Pete enters from right, followed by Backstab Bill and Cannibal Ike; they swagger to center stage as Snowball growls and cringes and Nellie takes off her apron and straightens her hair.)

PIG-EAR PETE:

    Good morning, dear lady, fine greetings
    On this beautiful December day.
    We've heard you have rooms for broke miners
    And if so, then we'd like to stay.

(Pig-Ear Pete, Backstab Bill and Cannibal Ike take off hats and bow to Nellie.)

PIG-EAR PETE:

    Pig-Ear Pete is the handle I carry;
    That's Backstab Bill and Cannibal Ike.
    And despite our unkempt appearance,
    We're the nicest gents come down the pike.

SNOWBALL: *(to audience from under table)*

    There's something that smells sort of fishy
    About this weasel-faced crew.
    I'd better stand guard in the kitchen,
    Or they might run off with the stew!

NELLIE: *(curtsies)*

    It's a pleasure to make your acquaintance,
    And of course, you may stay here awhile.
    We always have room for the weary,
    And we always have time for a smile.

PIG-EAR PETE: *(sidles close to Nellie)*

    Miss Nellie, your beauty is radiant;
    Your eyes shine like stars so bright.
    If only I'd found gold dust at Klondike,
    I'd court you from morning to night

SNOWBALL: *(to audience)*

    This fellow is so full of flattery,
    It practically runs out his ears.
    And worse, the smell from his britches
    Is bringing me close to tears!

NELLIE: *(giggles)*
>Now, surely, kind sir, you have money
>To keep you from rack and from ruin?

SNOWBALL: *(to Nellie)*
>Woof! Don't credit this liar!
>He's no more than a talking baboon!

BACKSTAB BILL:
>Dear lady, our story is woeful;
>We barely escaped with our lives.
>When that blue norther came through the valley,
>The wind cut the air like knives.

CANNIBAL IKE:
>We'd been digging for gold by Bonanza,
>Seeking our fortunes to find.
>There was light at the end of the mine shaft;
>The glitter near made me go blind!

BACKSTAB BILL:
>But then the landslide came crashing;
>Fifty tons of tumbling snow
>Roaring down the mountain
>On us poor miners below.

CANNIBAL IKE:
>We hadn't a chance but somehow survived
>Just by the skin of our teeth.
>But our hopes, our dreams, our precious stake
>Lay buried two miles beneath.

PIG-EAR PETE:
>That's not the worst we have to tell,
>Oh, the worst has not been told!
>For when we started back for home
>The weather turned really cold!
> Our sleds froze into the ground;
>Our eyes froze down to slits.
>Every time you said a word,
>It froze and cracked to bits.
> Birds froze solid on the wing;
>As did our shadows, head to toe.
>The wind itself got so darn cold,
>It couldn't even blow.

Oh, we were surely done for
When a miracle come our way—
The sun froze up and burst apart
Like a firecracker on Independence Day!
A million little sundrops
Spattered to the earth
And set the world back into motion
A-scrambling for all she's worth!

NELLIE:
My goodness, you men must be tired!
Why don't you relax or take a tour?
I've got to go on a short errand
And gather some goods for the poor. *(exits left)*

BACKSTAB BILL: *(to Pig-Ear Pete)*
Hey, boss, your plan's already working;
She's stuck like gum on a shoe.

CANNIBAL IKE:
Hey, watch what you're saying, you dimwit!
You'll give the whole world a clue!

PIG-EAR PETE:
Don't worry, boys, we're in clover;
This caper's a cinch to boot.
We'll wait till she goes to her claim site,
Then help ourselves to the loot.

(Pig-Ear Pete, Backstab Bill and Cannibal Ike snicker and exit left; Snowball comes out from table and addresses audience.)

SNOWBALL: *(to audience)*
I knew they were to up to trickery;
They couldn't fool even a cat.
But they'd better be sharp on the lookout—
Old Snowball will curry them flat! *(exits left)*
(LIGHTS OUT; Polar Bears enter and position themselves up left; table is removed behind scrim; "Moon Creek Mine" sign is placed at down left-center.)

SOURDOUGH SAM:

    You see, gold makes some folks plumb crazy;
    They forget what's wrong and what's right
    But, oh, these low-minded outlaws
    Were in for a whale of a fright!

    (LIGHTS FADE UP SLOWLY CENTER as Pig-Ear Pete,
    Backstab Bill and Cannibal Ike stumble out from left, looking
    lost; Pig-Ear Pete carries a map and stops to consult it;
    Backstab Bill and Cannibal Ike bump into him.)

PIG-EAR PETE:

    Watch where you're going, you varmints!
    You'll get us lost and confused!

BACKSTAB BILL:

    Say, let's ask those Ingaliks fishing;
    I bet they can give us some news.

    (LIGHTS UP RIGHT on Two Ingalik Indians sitting on large
    rock down right, fishing peacefully by the edge of a stream;
    Pig-Ear Pete, Backstab Bill and Cannibal Ike cross to them.)

INGALIK #1:

    Here come more foolish cheechakos,
    Their eyes glazed over with greed.

INGALIK #2:

    When will they learn their lesson
    And abide by nature's creed?

PIG-EAR PETE:

    Have you gents seen any treasure?
    Big claimings or maybe a mine?

CANNIBAL IKE:

    If you steer us the right direction,
    We'll give you a cut of our find.

INGALIK #1:

    Yes, we have seen plenty treasure;
    We see it right here every day.
    Caribou, beaver and otter;
    Moose and young gophers at play.

INGALIK #2:

    The forest is filled with good hunting
    And the most wondrous selection of herbs—
    Berries, wild onions and rhubarb,
    Sweet spruce gum for soothing your nerves.

INGALIK #1:

    You walk in a world of riches—
    Paradise right at your touch.

INGALIK #2:

    If that is the treasure you're seeking,
    The Great Spirit has given you much.

(Pig-Ear Pete, Backstab Bill and Cannibal Ike look at each other, exchange puzzled glances, shrug shoulders and wave goodbye to the Ingaliks.)

PIG-EAR PETE, BACKSTAB BILL & CANNIBAL IKE:

    Seeeeeeeeeee you later, alligators!

(LIGHTS FADE DOWN RIGHT, Ingaliks exit right; Pig-Ear Pete, Backstab Bill and Cannibal Ike turn and see Nellie and Snowball—carrying a picnic basket in his mouth—enter left and go up left and stand in front of what appear to be several large snow mounds; Pig-Ear Pete, Backstab Bill and Cannibal Ike duck down and eavesdrop, creeping slowly toward Nellie and Snowball.)

SOURDOUGH SAM:

    Nellie had come to her gold mine
    By the water's gentle flow.
    It was here she got fresh nuggets
    To give to poor miners below.

NELLIE:

    Oh, what a glorious beauty!
    These woods are so full of life!
    So quiet, so calm and so peaceful,
    Far away from all worldly strife.

(Nellie takes basket from Snowball and picks up gold

nuggets from the ground, putting them into basket; Snowball sniffs loudly and looks warily about.)

SNOWBALL:
    I smell a rat, dear mistress—
    The two-footed kind, the worst!
    Before we go any further,
    We had better check carefully first.

(Pig-Ear Pete, Backstab Bill and Cannibal Ike jump up and surprise Nellie and Snowball; Backstab Bill grabs basket from Nellie and slavers over the nuggets, Cannibal Ike taunts the barking Snowball with a glove, Pig-Ear Pete waves around a pistol .)

NELLIE:
    Dear fellows, your rudeness is shocking!
    Who taught you such manners as these?
CANNIBAL IKE:
    We thought we'd just help with your shopping—
BACKSTAB BILL: *(holds up a nugget)*
    And help ourselves as we please!
SNOWBALL: *(runs up to Pig-Ear Pete, barks twice)*
    I command you to cease right this moment!
    I command by the River Chilkoot!
    Or I, a fierce Yukon husky,
    Will chew your legs down to the root! *(barks twice)*

(Backstab Bill sits on snow mound #1; Cannibal Ike sits on snow mound #3.)

NELLIE: *(to Pig-Ear Pete)*
    Good sir, I feel I must warn you—
    You're in danger quite severe.
PIG-EAR PETE: *(laughs, waves pistol and sits down on snow mound #2)*
    As long I've got this six-shooter,
    There's nothing I have to fear.
    For might makes right,

CANNIBAL IKE:
    And we've got might,
BACKSTAB BILL: *(holds out basket)*
    So just put all your money right here!

(The snow mound under Pig-Ear Pete moves and stops; he double-takes, looks at it in disbelief; it moves again and flips him off. The snow mounds under Cannibal Ike and Backstab Bill also move, and they scramble off in terror and roll on ground. Abruptly, the snow mounds rise up, shake off their coat of snow and roar loudly—they are grumpy polar bears awakened from hibernation; Pig-Ear Pete, Backstab Bill and Cannibal Ike cringe in fear and crawl together in a circle hemmed in by bears.)

CANNIBAL IKE:
    Good glory, these ghosts are gigantic!
BACKSTAB BILL:
    With big furry paws and red tongues!
PIG-EAR PETE: *(waves pistol)*
    Don't worry, we've got them outnumbered;
    As long as I'm holding this gun!

(Polar Bear #1 steps forward, bows politely, and puts out his paw indicating he wants Pig-Ear Pete to place the gun there. Pig-Ear Pete points to himself questioningly.)

PIG-EAR PETE:
    Moi?

(Polar Bear #1 nods head "yes" and points to his outstretched paw with his other paw; Pig-Ear Pete gulps hard and daintily places gun in bear's paw; bear nods "thank you" and holds up gun for all to see, then bends it into a shapeless mass and thrusts it back at Pig-Ear Pete.)

POLAR BEAR #1:
    There you go, my dear fellow;
    Now no one shall be hurt.

POLAR #2:

Except for you thieving claim jumpers—

POLAR BEAR #3:

Who will shortly be pushing up dirt.

POLAR BEAR #4: *(puts paw on head of Backstab Bill)*

Hey, mom, you said I could eat one!

I like the heads the best!

POLAR BEAR #5: *(pulls Cannibal Ike up by one foot)*

I like to start with the toesies—

POLAR BEAR #6: *(pulls up Cannibal Ike's other foot)*

And I eat up all the rest!

NELLIE: *(steps forward)*

Wait, kind creatures of the mountain—

There's no need to be harsh or cruel,

For although these humans act beastly

We must remember the Golden Rule.

SNOWBALL:

Oh, come on, come on, dear mistress!

These bums should be hung out to dry!

I'd love to see them as mincemeat

Or cooked in a pizza pie!

POLAR BEAR #1:

Miss Nellie is right as always;

We must by her wishes abide.

(Polar Bear #2 grabs Pig-Ear Pete by the collar and tosses him toward stage right.)

POLAR BEAR #2:

But if she wasn't here to stop me,

I'd be barbecuing your hide!

(Polar Bear #3 grabs and tosses Backstab Bill; Polar Bear #4 grabs and tosses Cannibal Ike; villains dash offstage right, Snowball barking at their heels, then trotting back to center stage, where he sits.)

POLAR BEAR #5:

We still have six months to go

Before our winter sleep is through. *(yawns)*

(Polar Bears return to original places and begin settling down into mound positions; Nellie retrieves basket and she and Snowball amble offstage right, waving goodbye to bears.)

POLAR BEAR #6:
> We sure enjoyed the visit
> And hope you liked it, too.

POLAR BEAR #3:
> Miss Nellie Cashman, you're the tops;
> Be sure to hurry back.

POLAR BEAR #4:
> And the very next time you happen by—*(roars)*
> Don't forget to bring a snack!

(Bears pull covers over themselves and hibernate; Sourdough Sam strolls to center stage.)

SOURDOUGH SAM:
> Now there's the story of the goings-on
> That happened at Moon Creek Mine.
> When Pig-Ear Pete and his knavish crew
> Made their foray into crime.
>
> But Miss Nellie had a heart so true,
> It shone brighter than the purest gold
> And kept her safe from hurt and harm
> Till she stood at heaven's threshold.
>
> So, you folks with Klondike fever,
> One word of caution before you go—
> Don't sell your soul for a pot of gold
> And don't sit on just any...mound of snow.

(LIGHTS OUT.)

* THE END *

THE LITTLE OLD SOD SHANTY

After the Civil War, hundreds of thousands of settlers from around the world swarmed onto the Great Plains, many of them land-hungry farmers eager to begin cultivating acreage received from the Homestead Act of 1862. Life for these homesteaders, or "sodbusters" as they were often called, was not easy. The vast plains had almost no trees to use for timber, and the weather was extreme, ranging from bone-chilling blizzards to sweltering droughts; attacks of locusts, grasshoppers and other crop-killing insects were common. Yet many homesteaders stuck it out; improvements in farm machinery soon made it possible for a single farm family to harvest as much as 100 acres, and by 1890 the Great Plains had become the largest food-producing region of the world.

TIME: 1890

PLACE: A prairie homestead, Western North Dakota

CAST: 14 actors, min. 6 boys, 4 girls

Sadie Givens, age 46	Liza Cochran, age 23
Congressman	2 Railroad Agents
Hans Niethammer	Hilda Niethammer
Karl Niethammer	Lotte Niethammer
Sodbuster Pete	4 Square Dancers

RUNNING TIME: 20 minutes

STAGE SET: a rocking chair, a straight-backed wooden chair, one-room sod shanty measuring approximately six feet square

PROPS: shirt, sewing needle, purse, notebook, pencil, proclamation, 2 suitcases, coupon, sod trowel, butter churn, hoe,
stuffed chicken

MUSIC: *The Little Old Sod Shanty*, *The Lane County Bachelor*,
Dakota Land, *Skip to My Lou*

COSTUMES: Characters dress according to occupation—Sadie
Givens dresses in a plain farm dress and bonne, Liza Cochran
wears a city dress and hat, Sodbuster Pete wears overalls and
big work boots, etc.

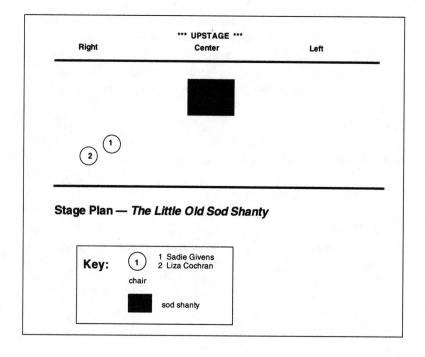

Stage Plan — *The Little Old Sod Shanty*

Key: ① 1 Sadie Givens
2 Liza Cochran
chair

■ sod shanty

(LIGHTS UP RIGHT on Sadie Givens sitting on a rocking chair at down right, sewing a shirt and softly singing. MUSIC: "The Little Old Sod Shanty.")

SADIE GIVENS: *(SINGS)*
Safely sheltered from the blizzards
and all the storms that came
In my little old sod shanty in the West

(Liza Cochran enters from right, carrying a purse; Sadie greets her.)

SADIE GIVENS: Hello there! You must be that newspaper reporter from back East!

LIZA COCHRAN: Liza Cochran from the *Pittsburgh Dispatch*.

SADIE GIVENS: My name is Sadie Givens, and welcome to our prairie homestead. Two hundred acres, all of it our own. Take a seat, dear. My youngest girl just made the cushion last night.

LIZA COCHRAN: *(sits in chair)* Thank you. That was very thoughtful.

SADIE GIVENS: It wasn't just thoughtful, Miss Cochran. It was practical. Out here on the prairie, if you want something, you make it or grow it yourself. It's been that way since my late husband Ellis and I first came out here twenty years ago, and I reckon it will be that way when they put me to bed with a pick and shovel.

LIZA COCHRAN: *(pulls pencil and notebook from purse)* My readers in the East want to know what life on a prairie homestead was like in the early days.

SADIE GIVENS: Have you ever been at sea, Miss Cochran?

LIZA COCHRAN: On the ocean? Of course, I sailed to London three years ago to report on Queen Victoria's Golden Jubilee.

SADIE GIVENS: *(stands, points out at audience)* Well, when we came here, this was all one big ocean. An ocean of grass. Thousands of years ago, great glaciers covered the Western Plains. After the glaciers melted, they left lakes and rivers and some of the best soil for growing anything in the world.

LIZA COCHRAN: Inculding grass?

SADIE GIVENS: When the first white settlers arrived in the early 1800s, ninety-eight per cent of North Dakota was nothing but grass as far as the eye could see. Why, the grass grew six feet high or more! There was all breeds of grass—bluestem and porcupine grass, switchgrass, junegrass and blue gramma, cordgrass and green needlegrass, threadleaf sedge and bearded wheatgrass, prairie dropseed—I could go on from now till next Sunday!

LIZA COCHRAN: Surely you and your husband didn't come to harvest grass?

SADIE GIVENS: *(sits)* Where Ellis and I grew up in southern Ohio, all the farming land had been taken. But the federal government wanted folks from the East to settle the Western Plains. So Congress started giving away land.

(LIGHTS UP LEFT on Congressman who stands down left and reads from proclamation.)

CONGRESSMAN: Under the Homestead Act of 1862, a settler will be given 160 acres of free land—called a "homestead"—provided he live on the land and cultivate a portion of it for five years. And, according to the Timber Culture Act of 1873, a settler may receive 160 acres of land by planting ten acres of trees.

(Congressman exits left; LIGHTS OUT LEFT.)

LIZA COCHRAN: That was very generous.

SADIE GIVENS: They were even more generous to the railroads. Why, the Northern Pacific Railroad got over fifty million acres of free land from Congress in 1864. The railroads advertised back East and all over Europe as far as Russia for folks to ride out West and settle the Plains.

(LIGHTS UP LEFT on Two Railroad Agents; Hans and Hilda Niethammer enter from left, dragging suitcases, and are accosted by the Railroad Agents.)

RAILROAD AGENT #1: Step right up, folks, step right up! *(shakes hands vigorously with Hans and Hilda)* The Great Plains and Rocky Mountain Railroad welcomes you to Chicago! Not planning to stick around this dumpy old burg long, are you?

RAILROAD AGENT #2: Let us give you a hand with your baggage. *(takes suitcases)* Where are you folks from?

HANS NIETHAMMER: My name is Hans Niethammer, and this is my vife, Hilda. Ve are from Germany.

HILDA NIETHAMMER: Ja, and ve have come a long way for some good crop land.

RAILROAD AGENT #1: Well, madam, you have come to the right place! Why, out in Dakota Territory, you plant a few taters and some Indian corn, and you'll need an ox team to pull the harvest out of the ground!

RAILROAD AGENT #2: *(puts arm around Hans' shoulder)* One morning a man named Ferguson dropped a few cucumber mango seeds in his front yard. Now, the cucumber mango is a fruit that is not native to these parts, as you might concur. Well, our friend Ferguson was considerable tired after his morning chores, so he took a stretch underneath the grove of lovely maple trees that cover his homestead and took a nap. Stranger, as true as I am talking to you this very blessed minute, when Farmer Ferguson awoke, he was tied fast to the tree! The cucumber mango vines had grown so high and thick and twisted around him while he slept, that he was completely bound as if by the coils of Medusa herself!

HILDA NIETHAMMER: That is incredible!

RAILROAD AGENT #1: And that's not all. Dakota Land is a paradise, folks. The flowers bloom ten months out of the year. Oranges and lemons and coconuts burst forth every week or so, and it's the only place in the country where the moon is always full.

RAILROAD AGENT #2: And best of all, folks, the land is filled with thrifty, healthy, moral people. In fact, it's so healthy, people rarely ever die, except from accident or old age. You folks aren't much past thirty, are you?

HANS NIETHAMMER: Is there a good supply of water in this Dakota?

RAILROAD AGENT #1: Friends, underneath the entire Dakota Territory, but especially where *your* land lies, is an immense boiling spring that discharges its overflow directly into the lake.

RAILROAD AGENT #2: Now, the specific gravity of the water in the hot springs is less than that of the lake, owing to the expansive action of heat. This water floats three or four feet thick upon the cold lake water underneath. You follow me?

RAILROAD AGENT #1: When you are in need of fresh fish, you cast your line through the hot upper stream, then you let your bait fall to the lake water below.

RAILROAD AGENT #2: You can catch your dinner and have it cooked on the way up! *(hands Hans Niethammer a coupon)* Here is a coupon for a ten per cent discount on your first one hundred miles of travel on the Great Plains and Rocky Mountain Railroad.

(Hans and Hilda walk to mid center as Railroad Agents wave farewell and sing. MUSIC: "Dakota Land.")

RAILROAD AGENT #1: *(SINGS)*
You soon will reach Dakota Land
Where plenty grows for folks to eat
RAILROAD AGENT #2: *(SINGS)*
The wind that blows forever sweet
In all the world is hard to beat
RAILROAD AGENTS #1 & 2: *(SING)*
Dakota land, sweet Dakota land
As on your lovely soil I stand
And look away across the plains
And wonder at the miles of grain

(LIGHTS OUT LEFT; Railroad Agents exit.)

SADIE GIVENS: Oh, the tales they told! But it worked. Folks from all over the world poured onto the Western Plains. Why, between 1878 and 1890 the population here in North Dakota grew from 16,000 to almost 200,000—and that's not including the 7,000 or so Sioux and Ojibway Indians who were here when we came and now live on reservations.

LIZA COCHRAN: But the things the railroad advertisements said about the rich soil and wonderful climate and plentiful water— what did folks do when they found out it wasn't true?

SADIE GIVENS: The same thing Ellis and I did. *(laughs)* We gritted our teeth, rolled our sleeves and stuck it out!

(LIGHTS UP CENTER on Hans and Hilda Niethammer and their two children, Karl and Lotte, somberly standing facing audience in front of a one-room sod shanty; Hans holds a sod trowel, Hilda a butter churn, Karl a hoe, Lotte a chicken.)

SADIE GIVENS: First, you make yourself a home. You dig strips of good old prairie earth—they call it sod—and pile them up until you've got a one-room hut with a chimney in the roof and maybe a window or two for a breath of fresh air now and again. Some folks cover the sod walls with boards they hauled in from back East and painted white, but after working eighteen hours a day for two weeks to put a roof over our heads, Ellis and I weren't feeling that fancy.

(MUSIC: "Dakota Land.")

HILDA NIETHAMMER: *(SINGS)*
    We have reached the land of drought and heat
    Where nothing grows for folks to eat
HANS NIETHAMMER: *(SINGS)*
    The wind that blows this awful heat
    In all the world is hard to beat
ALL NIETHAMMERS: *(SING)*
    Dakota land, sweet Dakota land
    As on your burning soil I stand
    And look away across the plains
    And wonder why it never rains

(Sodbuster Pete has entered from left during the song and watches Hilda, Karl and Lotte doing their chores and Hans trimming the shanty with the sod trowel.)

SODBUSTER PETE: Howdy, folks! Sodbuster Pete is my name. I'm your next door neighbor—just ten miles down the road. I'd be happy to give you a hand with that fine sod shanty you're a-building!

HANS NIETHAMMER: *(shakes Sodbuster Pete's hand)* Danke, Herr Pete. Danke. The railroad agents told us our land was in the middle of a forest. Did he mean a forest of grass?

SODBUSTER PETE: Haw-haw-haw! They're great jokers, those railroad fellers are! Listen, pard, life on a prairie homestead is no bucket of grins. You and your whole family work from sun up to sun down. You freeze in the winter, bake in the summer, and no matter what those folks back East tell you—there's not *ever* enough rain for your wheat crop!

HANS NIETHAMMER: Ja, Herr Pete. But this land...it is our *own* land.

(Hilda, Karl and Lotte gather beside Hans and hold hands.)

HILDA NIETHAMMER: And that is why we came to America. To work for ourselves—not for a duke or a king. Even if we starve to death, it is a choice we freely make!

SODBUSTER PETE: Well, folks, if it's freedom you want, you sure came to the right place.

(MUSIC: "The Lane County Bachelor.")

SODBUSTER PETE: *(SINGS)*
My name is Pete Bole, an old bachelor I am
I'm keeping a home on an elegant plan
You'll find me out West in the County of Lane
Starving to death on a government claim

KARL & LOTTE: *(SING)*
Hurrah for Lane County, the land of the free
The home of the grasshopper, bedbug and flea
I'll sing loud her praises and boast of her fame
While starving to death on a government claim

SODBUSTER PETE: *(SINGS)*
My house it is built of the natural soil
The walls are erected according to Hoyle
The roof has no pitch but is level and plain
And I always get wet when it happens to rain

HANS & HILDA: *(SING)*
Hurrah for Lane County, where blizzards arise
Where the winds never cease and the flea never dies
Where the sun is so hot if in it you remain
'Twill burn you to death on your government claim

SODBUSTER PETE: *(SINGS)*

> How happy I am when I crawl into bed
> And a rattlesnake rattles his tail at my head
> And the gay little centipede, void of all fear
> Crawls over my pillow and into my ear

KARL & LOTTE: *(SING)*

> So come to Lane County, there's room for you all

HANS & HILDA: *(SING)*

> Where the winds never cease and the rains never fall

SODBUSTER PETE: *(SINGS)*

> Come join in the chorus and boast of her fame

SODBUSTER PETE & NIETHAMMERS: *(SING)*

> While starving to death on your government claim

(Hilda, Karl and Lotte return to chores; Sodbuster Pete helps Hans trim the shanty.)

SADIE GIVENS: A family homestead was its own self-contained world. Everything they had or wanted, they made or grew themselves. Men plowed the fields, planted the crops and cared for the livestock—they had to hunt if they wanted fresh meat. Women raised and canned vegetables, milked cows, churned butter, made clothes, hauled water, cooked and cleaned and baked and cared for the children. Some women even homesteaded all by their lonesome—like me after Ellis passed away from the scarlet fever the second winter we were here.

LOTTE NIETHAMMER: *(to audience)* On our prairie homestead, each day of the week was a special day. There was Baking Day, when Mama did all the baking for the week. There was Mending Day, when all the mending was done. I helped with that.

KARL NIETHAMMER: Me, too!

LOTTE NIETHAMMER: And there was Washing Day, Ironing Day, Tool Repair Day—

KARL NIETHAMMER: Homestead children did a full day's work as soon as they could walk.

SADIE GIVENS: But homestead life wasn't all was hard work. In good weather, families would meet at a neighbor's homestead and have a big supper and a dance.

(Four Square Dancers enter from left and form a square at center; Sodbuster Pete assumes role of dance caller, as the Niethammers stand around the dancers and clap hands in rhythm. Music begins, dancers start dancing. MUSIC: "Skip to My Lou.")

SODBUSTER PETE: *(SINGS)*
Lou, lou, skip to my lou
Lou, lou, skip to my lou
Lou, lou, skip to my lou
Skip to my lou, my darling

KARL: *(SINGS)*
Little red wagon, paint it blue
Little red wagon, paint it blue
Little red wagon, paint it blue

LOTTE: *(SINGS)*
Skip to my lou, my darling

SODBUSTER PETE: *(SINGS)*
Fly's in the buttermilk, shoo, fly, shoo
Fly's in the buttermilk, shoo, fly, shoo
Fly's in the buttermilk, shoo, fly, shoo

SODBUSTER PETE & NIETHAMMERS: *(SING)*
Skip to my lou, my darling

HILDA: *(SINGS)*
Cows in the wheatfield, two by two
Cows in the wheatfield, two by two
Cows in the wheatfield, two by two

HANS: *(SINGS)*
Skip to my lou, my darling

SODBUSTER PETE & NIETHAMMERS: *(SING)*
Lou, lou, skip to my lou
Lou, lou, skip to my lou
Lou, lou, skip to my lou
Skip to my lou, my darling

(Dancers stop and everyone applauds.)

SADIE GIVENS: North Dakota became the 39th state last year on November 2, 1889—that's my birthday, don't you know.

LIZA COCHRAN: Congratulations, Miss Givens! I guess you're going stay on the prairie, then.

SADIE GIVENS: I wouldn't live anywhere else! *(points toward audience)* The future of America is right out there—in that endless sea of grass. After all, the word "Dakota" is a Sioux Indian word that means "allies"—friends and partners working together to build a better future. *(to Liza Cochran)* And you can quote me on that!

(All characters enter from left and stand at center in front of sod shanty; Sadie Givens and Liza Cochran stand and join others at center. MUSIC: "The Little Old Sod Shanty.")

SADIE GIVENS: *(SINGS)*
    You may sing about great mansions on gilded tree-lined lanes
    Or of European castles by the sea
SADIE GIVENS & LIZA COCHRAN: *(SING)*
    But my little old sod shanty that I built upon my claim
    Has become the dearest spot on earth to me
ALL CHARACTERS: *(SING)*
    I built it in my poverty upon my prairie claim
    And after toil it gave me sweetest rest
    Safely sheltered from the blizzards and all the storms of life
    In my little old sod shanty in the West

(LIGHTS OUT.)

* THE END *

The Little Old Sod Shanty
(traditional, arranged by L.E. McCullough)

You may sing a- bout great man- sions on gild- ed tree- lined

lanes or of Eur- o- pe- an cast- les by the sea

But my lit- tle old sod shan- ty that I built u- pon my

claim has be- come the dear- est spot on earth to me

I built it in my po- ver- ty u- pon my prair-ie

claim and af- ter toil it gave me sweet- est rest

Safe- ly shel- tered from the blizz- ards and all the storms of

life in my lit- tle old sod shan- ty in the West

The Lane County Bachelor
(traditional, arranged by L.E. McCullough)

My name is Pete Bole, an old bach-elor I am; I'm keep-ing a home on an el- e- gant plan; You'll find me out West in the Coun-ty of Lane, star-ving to death on a go-vern-ment claim. Hur-rah for Lane Coun-ty, the land of the free; the home of the grass-hop-per bed-bug and flea; I'll sing loud her prais- es and boast of her fame, while star- ving to death on a go-vern- ment claim

Dakota Land

(traditional, arranged by L.E. McCullough)

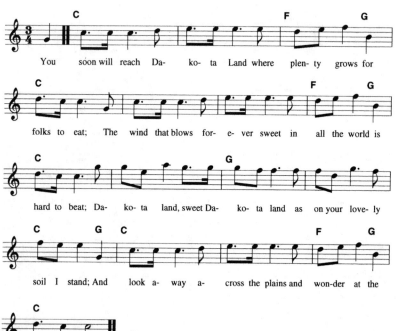

You soon will reach Da- ko- ta Land where plen- ty grows for

folks to eat; The wind that blows for- e- ver sweet in all the world is

hard to beat; Da- ko- ta land, sweet Da- ko- ta land as on your love- ly

soil I stand; And look a- way a- cross the plains and won-der at the

miles of grain

Skip to My Lou

(traditional, arranged by L.E. McCullough)

Lou, lou, skip to my lou; Lou, lou, skip to my lou;

Lou, lou, skip to my lou; Skip to my lou, my dar- ling

Lit- tle red wa-gon, paint it blue; Lit- tle red wa- gon, paint it blue;

Lit- tle red wa-gon, paint it blue; Skip to my lou, my dar- ling

EL PASEO DEL VAQUERO
(THE RIDE OF THE VAQUERO)

Popular culture gives the impression that the cowboy is a strictly American, late 1800s figure. However, the first cattle arrived in the Western Hemisphere from Spain in 1494 and spread throughout the West Indies, Mexico and Central and South America before reaching north of the Rio Grande River into the present-day United States. Mexican cowboys, or *vaqueros* as they were known, helped create the modern cowboy as we know him, contributing their craft, lore and language of cattle herding to their *norte americano* brothers. Historians estimate that during the twenty years after the Civil War, when the U.S. cattle industry was at its peak, over 40,000 cowboys roamed the ranges of the American West with their bovine charges; in 1885 forty-four per cent of land in the United States was devoted to raising cattle.

TIME: 1890; 1850

PLACE: Chicago, Illinois; Sante Fe, New Mexico

CAST: 15 actors, min. 9 boys, 3 girls

Harvey	Hannah
Mike Hoskins, Age 50	Mike Hoskins, Age 10
Felipe Ortiz	Carlos Robledo
Pedro Garcia	Padre Montoya
2 Aztecs	2 Cattle
Pueblo Man	Pueblo Woman
Mike's Mother	

RUNNING TIME: 20 minutes

STAGE SET: stool at down right, four-foot length of corral fence at mid center with a small crate to the fence's right

PROPS: 4 lariats, 2 herding sticks, parchment scroll, writing quill, sombrero, bandana, pair of chaps, chaqueta, pair of gloves, pair of boots, tortilla, bowl, piece of leather, 2 spurs

MUSIC: *Old Paint, Cielito Lindo, El Toro Prieto*

COSTUMES: Harvey and Hannah dress as late 19th-century city children; Mike Hoskins, Age 50 wears "citified" cowboy garb— short-brimmed Stetson, colored neckerchief, bib pullover shirt, Levi pants, knee-length boots; Mike Hoskins, Age 10 dresses as mid-19th-century rural boy; Los Vaqueros wear vaquero clothing as described in play; Aztecs and Pueblos wear tribal dress; Cattle wear masks, horns, brown or black body-covering

(LIGHTS UP RIGHT on Harvey at down right, standing in front of a stool and trying to twirl a rope as if it were a lariat. Hannah enters from left and crosses slowly to center without Harvey noticing her.)

HARVEY: Yee-haw! Ride 'em, cowboy! Saddle up, you bronc busters! Yee-haw! Whoops!

(Harvey tangles himself up in the rope.)

HANNAH: Some cowboy you are, Harvey Hoskins! Hasn't anybody told you they don't have cattle drives in Chicago?

HARVEY: They used to! Once in 1854, all the way from Texas!

HANNAH: Says who?

HARVEY: Says my Uncle Mike! He's visiting us for a week, and he's from out West.

HANNAH: Your Uncle Mike and my Aunt Gerty! What would *he* know about cattle drives?

HARVEY: He'd know a lot! He was a cowboy!

HANNAH: Sure he was! And you told me last week your Uncle Elwood invented a horseless carriage in Kokomo!

HARVEY: Well, he did, too! But, it ran out of gasoline.

(Uncle Mike enters from left and strolls toward center stage, singing. MUSIC: "Old Paint.")

UNCLE MIKE: *(SINGS)*
    My foot's in the stirrup, my pony won't stand
    Goodbye, Old Paint, I'm leavin' Cheyenne

HARVEY: Uncle Mike!

UNCLE MIKE: Good morning, Harvey! *(bows to Hannah)* Good morning, Miss.

HARVEY: Uncle Mike, this is Hannah, who lives next door and comes over to annoy me now and again. Hannah, this is my Uncle Mike—the *cowboy.*

HANNAH: *(grabs rope from Harvey)* Harvey says you're a real cowboy. Can you do a fancy rope trick?

UNCLE MIKE: *(takes rope, laughs heartily)* Haw-haw-haw! Little lady, I admire your spunk. But there is a lot more to being a cowboy than doing rope tricks. *(sits on stool)* Rest your haunches a spell, and I'll spin a yarn about the *real* cowboys of the West.

(LIGHTS OUT RIGHT; Felipe, Carlos and Pedro sings offstage left. MUSIC: "El Toro Prieto.")

FELIPE, CARLOS & PEDRO: *(SING, O.S.)*
    Aquí les voy a cantar
    del esto torito negrito
    voy a cantarle a las huellas
    del mentado toro prieto

(LIGHTS UP CENTER AND LEFT on three vaqueros—Felipe Ortiz, Carlos Robledo, Pedro Garcia—lounging in front of a corral fence at mid center with a small crate to the fence's right; Young Mike Hoskins enters from left and watches the vaqueros from a few feet away.)

UNCLE MIKE: *(O.S.)* It was forty years ago, in 1850. The war the United States had fought with Mexico had ended two years before, and California and New Mexico were now U.S. territories. I was just a scrap of a boy—ten years old and soaking wet behind both ears—when my parents moved from Windsor, Connecticut to Santa Fe, New Mexico. Father ran the office of the Overland Mail company, and mother taught school at what used to be a little Spanish mission. One day I wandered over to a pen where the stage horses were kept and saw three young men in their early twenties singing and laughing in Spanish.

YOUNG MIKE HOSKINS: *(approaches vaqueros and speaks in halting Spanish)* Bunn-us day-us, seen-yor-ays.

FELIPE: Buenas días, señor. ¿Cómo usted?

CARLOS: ¿Quién es usted?

PEDRO: ¿Es usted norteamericano?

YOUNG MIKE HOSKINS: Gosh, I...I don't reckon I speak Spanish as fast as you fellows.

FELIPE: Well, that is too bad, señor. Because we do not speak *any* English.

(Felipe, Carlos and Pedro laugh.)

CARLOS: He is just pulling your pierna.
YOUNG MIKE HOSKINS: My what?
FELIPE: Pierna—your leg.
PEDRO: *(bows)* Mi nombre es Pedro Garcia. My name is Pedro Garcia. Te presento mis amigos, Felipe Ortiz y Carlos Robledo.

(Felipe and Carlos bow as they are introduced.)

YOUNG MIKE HOSKINS: My name is Mike Hoskins. Are you coach drivers for the Overland Stage?

(Felipe, Carlos and Pedro laugh, then stand up straight and tall.)

FELIPE: No, señor. We are not coach drivers.
CARLOS: ¡Somos vaqueros!
PEDRO: We are vaqueros!
YOUNG MIKE HOSKINS: What is a vaquero?

(Felipe, Carlos and Pedro exchange glances of surprise and amazement, then confer together for a few seconds.)

PEDRO: Venga usted aquí. Come here, Miguelito.

(Felipe and Carlos each take Young Mike Hoskins by an arm and steer him to Pedro, who points to audience.)

PEDRO: Look out there, Miguelito, to the south. You may see only a dusty trail leading to the purple mountains and to Mexico… but if you look hard enough, you can see El Paseo del Vaquero—The Ride of the Vaquero.

(Two Aztecs, each carrying a herding stick, enter from left and look around for cattle.)

FELIPE: The first cattle in the Americas were brought by Christopher Columbus on his second voyage to the New World from Spain. Gregorio de Villalobos brought cattle to Mexico in 1521, and within a few years cattle roamed everywhere throughout Mexico.

(Two Cattle enter from right and amble to down center.)

TWO CATTLE: Mooooo! Mooooo!

CARLOS: The Spanish conquistadors made slaves of the native people of Mexico, such as the Aztecs. It was Aztec slaves who were the first vaqueros. Their job was to watch the cattle—*las vacas*—and see that they did not wander too far away from *la hacienda*—the ranch.

(The Two Aztecs apprehend the Cattle and nudge them with sticks to exit left.)

PEDRO: After awhile, these men who kept track of *las vacadas*— the cattle herds—were called *vaqueros*. They became free men who worked for the rancher—*el hacendad*. And by the early 1600s they had a lot more work to do than just follow lost cows.

FELIPE: First, they needed proper working clothes. *(takes off his sombrero and shows it to Mike)* For the head—*el sombrero*, from the verb *sombrear*—to shade. It gets pretty hot in Mexico when you are out in the sun all day. So you need your own shade, a sombrero.

CARLOS: The first sombreros were made of woven palms. Now they are made from leather or felt, like Felipe's.

(Felipe takes his sombrero and puts it on Mike's head.)

PEDRO: And to protect your face from the wind and the dust, you better have a silk sash or *bandana*. *(unties a sash from his waist and ties it around Mike's neck)*

FELIPE: Of course, when you look for lost cattle, the cattle want to hide. Where do they hide? In the bushes that have big thorns that rip your legs, unless you wear *chaparejos* to cover them. *(takes a pair of chaps from crate and puts them around Mike's legs)* That's good leather, señor.

CARLOS: Good leather keeps out wind and water. Because a vaquero is going to spend most of his time in the saddle, in the weather. *(takes a pair of gloves from crate and hands them to Mike, who puts them on)* Better have strong gloves for pulling rope.

PEDRO: *(takes a leather chaqueta from crate and puts it around Mike's shoulders)* And a *chaqueta*—a jacket of leather to protect your arms when you tumble off your horse.

FELIPE: And *botas*—you must have a pair of leather boots to ride tall in the saddle. *(takes a pair of boots from crate and hands them to Mike, who puts them on)*

CARLOS: *(takes a pair of spurs from crate and holds them up)* And last but not at all least, *las espuelas*—the spurs. Spurs like this were worn by *los caballeros*—the great warrior knights of medieval Spain.

PEDRO: Spurs are the sign of a true vaquero!

FELIPE: ¡Mira! ¡Miguelito es un vaquero!

(Felipe, Carlos and Pedro laugh and applaud as Mike takes stock of his new clothes.)

CARLOS: Besides clothes, a vaquero must have the proper working tools. Because in Mexico and New Spain, cattle became very important, especially to the missions north of the Rio Grande.

(Padre Montoya enters from left, carrying a parchment scroll and a writing quill, and walks to down left; he is followed by an Pueblo Woman and Pueblo Man who flank him, kneeling; as Padre Montoya speaks, Pueblo Woman rolls a tortilla over a bowl and Pueblo Man braids a piece leather into a rope.)

PADRE MONTOYA: *(addresses audience)* Buenas días, niñas y niños. Mi nombre es Padre Montoya. I am the superior of La Misión de San Miguel here at Santa Fe, among the Pueblo tribe. Since we established the mission in 1636, we have become completely self-sufficient. We make and grow everything here—the adobe blocks that build our church and our homes, the corn our Indian women make into tortillas, the cloth woven by our Indian men into the simple clothes we wear. However, the most important material possession with which we are blessed, is our cattle.

PUEBLO WOMAN: From one cow, we can make soap to wash, candles to see and fat to cook our tortillas.

PUEBLO MAN: The hide of a cow is tanned and made into shoes, sandals, saddles, clothing, even door hinges. *(holds up leather)* And for the vaqueros who tend the cattle, we make the rope—*la reata.*

FELIPE, CARLOS & PEDRO: ¡La reata!

(Felipe, Carlos and Pedro each pull out a lariat and twirl it, singing. MUSIC: chorus of "Cielito Lindo." Padre Montoya, Pueblo Woman and Pueblo Man exit left.)

FELIPE, CARLOS & PEDRO: *(SING)*
¡Ay, ay, ay, ay!
¡Ay, reata bonita!

PEDRO: The reata—or "lariat" as they call it in English—is a vaquero's most precious tool. A good strong lariat can allow a little tiny hombre like Carlos to drag a one thousand pound bull to the branding fire.

(Carlos mimes dragging a bull.)

PEDRO: Or help Felipe save his horse from drowning in quicksand.

(Felipe mimes pulling a horse from quicksand.)

PEDRO: And when you sleep at night in the desert, you can put it around your head. *(puts lariat around Mike's head and toggles it lightly)*

YOUNG MIKE HOSKINS: Why is that?

PEDRO: To make sure you wake up, señor…because, as everyone knows, a rattlesnake will not cross a cowhair rope.

(Mike throws off lariat, and Felipe, Carlos and Pedro laugh; Felipe puts crate on end in front of Mike and sits him on it as Carlos hands his lariat to Mike and directs his gaze to audience.)

FELIPE: One day you are out on the range, high in the saddle…

CARLOS: You see a big bull running away from the herd…what are you going to do?

PEDRO: You turn your horse toward the bull…you take your lariat and get ready to throw it into the air…

(Mike twirls lariat.)

PEDRO: But you wait…

(Mike stops twirling lariat.)

PEDRO: And you think…

YOUNG MIKE HOSKINS: What kind of lasso am I going to use?

PEDRO: ¡Bueno! There are five ways a vaquero can lasso an animal. One is the "pitch," which is good for catching animals already in a corral. The loop of the lasso travels through the air horizontally, like this.

(Felipe twirls lariat horizontally.)

PEDRO: The second is the "slip," which is like the pitch but travels vertically, like this.

(Felipe twirls lariat vertically.)

CARLOS: Or you could use a "heeling" catch, where the lasso falls in front of the animal's legs.

(Felipe tosses lariat in front of him, then pulls quickly as if catching an animal.)

CARLOS: Vaqueros in California would catch grizzly bears with that one. But you are on a horse, so maybe the "backhand slip" is best. This takes much skill, because you have to throw the lasso behind you as you ride.
(Felipe turns back to audience and tosses lariat behind him, then turns and pulls quickly.)

PEDRO: Or maybe you should just use a "forefoot"—throw the lasso and catch the bull by its front legs.

(Mike throws lariat in front of him.)

FELIPE: The rope falls over the bull's shoulders, and you pull back very hard...

(Mike pulls back hard.)

CARLOS: You wrap your end of the lariat around your saddle horn with a half-hitch knot—quickly, or you will lose a finger when the bull dashes away!

(Mike wraps lariat around imaginary saddle horn and jerks back hard, miming a struggle with a bull.)

PEDRO: ¡Aguila! Watch out!
FELIPE: ¡No le afloje! Courage!

(Mike yanks the rope, jumps off the crate and bounds to down center, where he kneels on the ground as if he has just brought down the bull.)

CARLOS: You got him! ¡Muy excelente!

(Felipe, Carlos and Pedro shout and cheer, clap Mike on back.)

FELIPE, CARLOS & PEDRO: ¡Fantástico! ¡Qué genio! ¡Miguelito es un hombre bravo!
MIKE'S MOTHER: *(O.S.)* Michael! Come home for dinner! Michael!
YOUNG MIKE HOSKINS: *(rises, hands lariat back to Carlos)* That's my mother calling, so I better go. Thanks a lot, fellows! Being a vaquero sounds like a lot of fun!
FELIPE: It is a noble way of life.
CARLOS: As long as there are cattle to drive, there will be vaqueros to drive them.

PEDRO: (holds up spurs) And you, señor, can win your own spurs when you join El Paseo del Vaquero.

(Mike exits left.)

FELIPE, CARLOS & PEDRO: ¡Hasta la vista! See you later! ¡Adios, muchacho!

(LIGHTS OUT CENTER AND LEFT; LIGHTS UP RIGHT on Harvey, Hannah and Uncle Mike.)

HANNAH: So that's where cowboys come from?

UNCLE MIKE: Like the other American ranchers who settled in the Southwest, I learned the tricks of the cattle-driving trade from the Mexican vaqueros. Joined my first roundup at age fourteen and kept on the trail until a couple years ago.

HARVEY: Do they still have cattle drives out West?

UNCLE MIKE: Nowadays, the only cattle drives are herding steers from the pen to the railroad car that takes them to the city.

HANNAH: And the vaqueros? What happened to them?

UNCLE MIKE: I'm afraid they're just a memory, Miss Hannah. (looks out at audience) But when the moon shines a certain way, and the wind blows just right, you can hear them singing one of their wild songs, as they speed gaily along the trail—El Paseo del Vaquero.

(Uncle Mike, Harvey and Hannah sing as all other cast members enter from left and join in on chorus. MUSIC: "Cielito Lindo.")

UNCLE MIKE, HARVEY & HANNAH: (SING)
De la Sierra Morena
Cielito Lindo vienen bajando
Un par deojitos negros
Cielito Lindo, de contrabando
ALL: (SING)
Ay, ay, ay, ay!
Canta y no llores
Porque cantando sealegran
Cielito Lindo los corazones

Ay, ay, ay, ay!
Canta y no llores
Porque cantando sealegran
Cielito Lindo los corazones

(LIGHTS OUT.)

* THE END *

Old Paint

(traditional, arranged by L.E. McCullough)

My foot's in the stir- rup, my po- ny won't stand, Good-bye, Old Paint —— I'm leav- in' Chey- enne

El Toro Prieto

(traditional, arranged by L.E. McCullough)

A- quí les voy —— a can- tar

Del es- to to- ri- to ne- gri- to

Voy a can- tar- le a las hue- llas

Del men- ta- do to- ro pri- e- to

English Translation

Now I am going to sing to you
Of the little black bull;
I'm going to tell you all
About the famous black bull.

Cielito Lindo

(traditional, arranged by L.E. McCullough)

English Translation

From the Sierra Morena
A beautiful bit of heaven comes down
A pair of little black eyes
Beautiful bit of heaven, the forbidden.

Ay, ay, ay, ay!
Sing! No use crying!
For singing seals
A beautiful bit of heaven in our hearts.

PONY EXPRESS RIDER

Though the Pony Express only existed for a year and a half during 1860–61, it won a lasting place in American folklore and the history of the West. Able to cover nearly 2,000 miles in 10 days, the Pony Express carried letters from ordinary folks as well as important government and business documents—even England's Royal Navy sent mail from China through America with the Pony Express and then eastward to London. Pony Express riders were rugged and courageous; Bufflo Bill Cody was only 14 years old when he joined the Pony Express, and he had several close calls with hostile Indians and robbers. Eventually made obsolete by the telegraph and railroad, the Pony Express succeeded in delivering over 34,000 pieces of mail; its riders traveled a total mileage equal to circling 24 times around the world.

TIME: Present; May, 1860

PLACE: Present—a grade school classroom, Anytown, USA; Past—St. Joseph, Missouri

CAST: 18 actors, min. 5 boys, 3 girls

Tim	Tina
Ms. Lopez	Newsgirl
Bill Cody, age 14	Pat McEneaney, age 18
Alexander Majors	Stable Master Simms
3 Townsfolk	3 Bandits
4 Railroad Workers	

RUNNING TIME: 20 minutes

STAGE SET: 2 tables (one on which a computer work station sits), 2 chairs, a barrel, anvil

PROPS: computer, 3 newspapers, a pen, writing paper, black-smith's hammer, horse shoe, mailpouch,

EFFECTS: Sound—loud rhythmic hammer strikes

MUSIC: *Pony Express Rider*

COSTUMES: Tim, Tina and Ms. Lopez wear contemporary 1990s clothes; 1860 characters wear clothes appropriate to their occupation: Alexander Majors wears a suit; Stable Master Simms wears overalls; Townsfolk wears vests if male or long dresses if female; Bandits should be masked; Railroad Workers can wear overalls with peaked railroad caps; Bill Cody and Pat McEneaney each wear buckskin shirt, blue or black cloth trousers tucked into black or brown knee boots and a slouch hat

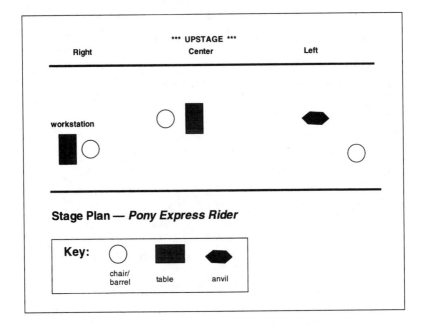

(LIGHTS UP RIGHT on Tim seated at a computer work station, with Tina standing next to him. Tim types rapidly, frustration growing.)

TIM: I can't believe it!

TINA: Oh no, is it doing it again?

TIM: I can't believe it!

TINA: *(stamps her foot)* Oh no, it's doing it again.

TIM: I can't believe it!

TINA: This is too much!

(The teacher, Ms. Lopez, enters from right and stands behind Tim and Tina, observing them.)

TIM: *(wrings hands)* I'm going to scream.

TINA: No, *I'm* going to scream.

TIM: *(rubs knuckles into his head)* Uh-uh—*I'm* going to scream.

TINA: No, you screamed last time. This time is *my* turn to scream.

MS. LOPEZ: Tim! Tina! What is wrong with you two? You're disrupting the rest of the computer lab!

TINA: I'm sorry, Ms. Lopez, but the modem froze up again—right when we were going to send e-mail to our partner class in Thailand.

TIM: Ms. Lopez, is it a crime to strangle a computer?

MS. LOPEZ: I'm sure the modem will straighten itself out. It isn't going to work any better with you two scowling at it.

TINA: Ms. Lopez is right, Tim. Let's give it a rest for a bit.

TIM: But our e-mail ought to be there *now!*

MS. LOPEZ: *(chuckles)* Always in such a hurry! Tim and Tina, you would have made perfect riders for the Pony Express.

TIM: The Pony Express? What's that?

TINA: I know. Wasn't the Pony Express a horse race in the old West?

MS. LOPEZ: It wasn't a race. It was a private postal service that promised customers it would get mail from Missouri to California in ten days.

TIM: *(snickers)* Ten days? I can get e-mail halfway around the world in less than ten seconds. *(frowns at computer)* When this thing *works!*

MS. LOPEZ: The Pony Express began on April 3, 1860. Back then, it tooks two months to get mail from New York to San Francisco by land. By ocean voyage it could take up to seven months.

TINA: The telegraph was invented in 1844. Couldn't people send messages with it?

MS. LOPEZ: Of course. But telegraph lines didn't run across the United States, especially west of the Mississippi River. If you wanted to send someone in California a private letter or a present, the telegraph wouldn't do. There was only the Pony Express.

(LIGHTS OUT RIGHT; LIGHTS UP LEFT on two teenage boys—Pat McEneaney and Bill Cody—one sitting on a barrel, the other standing. A Newsgirl enters from right hawking newspapers.)

NEWSGIRL: Extra! Extra! Republicans nominate Lincoln of Illinois for President! Get the latest news right here!

PAT MCENEANEY: Say there, newsie, let us have one of those ink catchers.

NEWSGIRL: It'll cost you three cents. If you have *that* much between the two of you.

PAT MCENEANEY: *(looks at Bill)* I've got a copper or my name isn't Pat McEneaney from the County Roscommon!

BILL CODY: *(digs hands into both pockets, pulls out a coin in each)* Two hapennies here.

PAT MCENEANEY: *(gives his and Bill's coins to Newsgirl)* How about if you lend us the third penny?

NEWSGIRL: *(pulls paper away)* Lend it?

PAT MCENEANEY : We're headed for the gold strike in Colorado. We'll be millionaires in a month, won't we, Bill Cody?

NEWSGIRL: Awwww, you're a couple of pikers! *(thrusts paper at Cody)* Here, find yourself a job! *(exits left)*

PAT MCENEANEY : *(bows, calls after her)* Thank you, thank you! May you marry a mule and have kittens! *(to Bill)* What's it say about the gold strike?

BILL CODY: *(peers at paper, frowns)* Gosh, Pat, I...well, let's see here...

PAT MCENEANEY: *(takes paper)* Give it over till I look. *(scans quickly)* Aha! Here's just what the doctor ordered: "Wanted— Young, skinny wiry fellows not over eighteen. Must be expert riders willing to risk death daily. Orphans preferred." That's us to a T!

BILL CODY: I don't know, Pat—we both ride pretty good. But I'm not an orphan. My mother is still alive in Kansas.

PAT MCENEANEY: *(takes Bill's arm)* Come along, Cody. Let's join the Pony Express and make our fortune!

(LIGHTS OUT LEFT; LIGHTS UP CENTER as Pat and Bill cross to mid-center stage and stand in front of a table, where Alexander Majors sits writing on papers; Pat clears his throat, and Majors looks up.)

PAT MCENEANEY: Are you Mister Alexander Majors of the Central Overland, California and Pike's Peak Express Company, the largest freight carrier in the nation and the operator of the Pony Express?

ALEXANDER MAJORS: It is and I am. What can I do for you?

PAT MCENEANEY : We want to join the Pony Express!

ALEXANDER MAJORS: You do, eh? Well, so do a lot of other young whipper snappers. What are your names and ages?

PAT MCENEANEY: Patrick Christopher Aloysius McEneaney. Age eighteen.

BILL CODY: William Frederick Cody, sir. Just turned fourteen February twenty-sixth.

ALEXANDER MAJORS: Well, you boys are the right size and age. But it's a man's job you're bucking for. The Pony Express carries the mail from St. Joe to Frisco—one thousand nine hundred sixty-six miles in ten days or less, *guaranteed*. Each rider travels fifty to seventy-five miles before passing the mail pouch to the relief rider at the next station. That's *if* the station hasn't been attacked and burnt down by Indians or robbed by bandits. And this is no Sunday school frolic—you'll ride through heat and snow, mountains and deserts, charging buffalo and hungry wolves, rain that'll drown you pink and dust that'll choke the guts right out of your stomach.

BILL CODY: Mister Alexander, I wasn't born in the woods to be scared by a hoot owl. I've been working since I was ten years old. I need this job awful bad.

PAT MCENEANEY: I've crossed an ocean to get this far. San Francisco or bust!

ALEXANDER MAJORS: I can see you boys are all boiled up and fit to be tied. Very well, you're hired. You'll get fifty dollars a month, plus board and keep.

(Pat and Bill shake hands and congratulate each other.)

PAT MCENEANEY: When do we start, Mister Majors?

ALEXANDER MAJORS: This afternoon. But first, you must take the official Pony Express oath. Raise your right hands and repeat after me.

(Pat raises his left hand.)

ALEXANDER MAJORS: *(clears throat)* Ahem.

(Bill nudges Pat, who realizes his error and raises his right hand.)

ALEXANDER MAJORS: While I am in the employ of the Pony Express...

BILL & PAT: While I am in the employ of the Pony Express...

ALEXANDER MAJORS: I agree not to use profane language...

BILL & PAT: I agree not to use profane language...

ALEXANDER MAJORS: Not to become inebriated...

BILL & PAT: Not to become inebriated...

ALEXANDER MAJORS: Not to place wagers...

BILL & PAT: Not to place wagers...

ALEXANDER MAJORS: Not to treat animals cruelly...

BILL & PAT: Not to treat animals cruelly...

ALEXANDER MAJORS: And not to do anything else incompatible with the conduct of a gentleman.

BILL & PAT: *(mumble)* Mmmmmmm, gentleman.

BILL CODY *(to Pat)*: What's all those ten-dollar words mean, Pat?

PAT MCENEANEY: It means you can't cuss, drink whiskey, play cards or beat a horse.

BILL CODY: Well, I wouldn't do any of those things anyhow.

ALEXANDER MAJORS: Excellent. Now, go to Number 12 Jules Street and see the stable master, Simms. He'll get you squared away.

PAT MCENEANEY: Thank you, sir. May your soul reach heaven an hour before the devil knows you're dead.

BILL CODY: Thank you, Mister Majors. You won't be sorry you took us on.

ALEXANDER MAJORS: *I* won't be. But *you* might.

(LIGHTS OUT CENTER; LIGHTS UP LEFT on Stable Master Simms at mid-left; he is behind an anvil hammering a horse shoe as Pat and Bill approach.)

PAT MCENEANEY: Stable Master Simms?

STABLE MASTER SIMMS: You're looking at him. And you must be the new riders. *(picks up a mailpouch and shows it to Pat and Bill)* Here's your *mochila*.

BILL CODY: Our what?

STABLE MASTER SIMMS: *Mochila. Mochila* is the Spanish word for knapsack. ¿Habla español, amigo?

PAT MCENEANEY: Begging your extreme pardon, Mister Simms, but if that's the Spanish word for knapsack, and we're all speaking English at the moment, why don't we just call it "the knapsack"?

STABLE MASTER SIMMS: Because *mochila* is what the man who made it calls it! It's a mailpouch designed by Israel Landis, the finest saddlemaker in all thirty-three States of the Union plus Mexico. The *mochila* and saddle together weigh just over twelve pounds, a third less than your regular saddle rig. That'll come in handy when you've been on the trail for half a day without food nor water.

BILL CODY: Do we carry our own grub?

STABLE MASTER SIMMS: Nope. That'll be at the next station, along with a fresh mount. And you've got just two minutes to change mounts. Remember: a Pony Express rider travels light as possible. *(grabs Pat's chin)* You better shave closer, son— you don't want any extra whiskers to weigh you down.

PAT MCENEANEY: It's not my whiskers I'm worried about keeping...it's my hair. *(runs fingers through hair)*

STABLE MASTER SIMMS: Oh, you mean Indians? Well, we didn't have any trouble at all, until some sodbusters in Paiute territory cut down all the trees near the reservation and ran off the buffalo. Those are the tribe's only source of food, so they got a mite riled.

PAT MCENEANEY: A mite riled?

STABLE MASTER SIMMS: Last week Pony Bob Haslam met up with some hostiles in Utah Territory. Got his jaw broke by an arrow and his arm busted by bullets. But, by juniper, he finished his run right on schedule!

PAT MCENEANEY: Lucky for him.

STATION MASTER SIMMS: Oh, quit your bellyaching! You boys don't have a thing to worry about. Indian horses feed on grass. Our horses feed on grain. Grain builds better muscles for the long run. Your horse will get you out of shooting range quicker than the Indians can fire. Now, take your *mochila* and pick your mounts. *(begins singing "Pony Express Rider" as LIGHTS FADE OUT LEFT)*

STABLEMASTER SIMMS: *(SINGS, O.S.)*
With a merry little jog and a merry little song
Whoa-ha! Buck and Jerry!
We're riding straight across the Western plains
Whoa-ha! Buck and Jerry!

STABLEMASTER SIMMS, ALL CAST EXCEPT
PAT & BILL: *(SING, O.S.)*
Pony Express rider! Pounding down the trail!
Pony Express rider! Bringing in the mail!

STABLEMASTER SIMMS: *(SINGS, O.S.)*
Though we are covered all over with dust
Whoa-ha! Buck and Jerry!
It's better than staying back home to rust
Whoa-ha! Buck and Jerry!

STABLEMASTER SIMMS, ALL CAST EXCEPT
PAT & BILL: *(SING, O.S.)*
Pony Express rider! Pounding down the trail!
Pony Express rider! Bringing in the mail!

(LIGHTS UP LEFT as Newsgirl enters from left followed by Three Townsfolk; Townsfolk #1 and #2 each take a paper from Newsgirl.)

NEWSGIRL: Extra! Extra! Pony Express Rider Makes Marathon Run! Get the latest news right here!

TOWNSFOLK #1: *(reads)* Bill Cody rides one hundred sixteen miles through Nebraska between Red Buttes and Three Crossings...

TOWNSFOLK #2: *(reads)* Only to arrive and find his replacement rider was killed the day before in a gunfight...

TOWNSFOLK #3: What'd he do? What'd he do?

NEWSGIRL: Extra! Extra! Read all about it!

TOWNSFOLK #1: *(reads)* He rides on another seventy-seven miles to Rocky Ridge...

TOWNSFOLK #2: *(reads)* Only to arrive and find the station has been burnt by renegades...

TOWNSFOLK #3: What'd he do? What'd he do?

NEWSGIRL: Extra! Extra! Read all about it!

TOWNSFOLK #1: *(reads)* He keeps on going to Mud Springs, eighty miles away...

TOWNSFOLK #2: *(reads)* But is waylaid by armed bandits who order him to hand over the mail pouch...

(LIGHTS OUT LEFT; LIGHTS UP CENTER on Bill Cody at mid-center; Three Bandits, each masked and bearing a pistol or rifle, stand around him.)

BILL CODY: Looks like you got the best of me, fellers. I reckon you want this *mochila*. *(swings mochila faster and faster)* Well, I want you to have it. Get ready, cause here it comes!

(He smacks them with the mochila; they fall down and he gallops offstage up right; LIGHTS OUT CENTER. MUSIC: "Pony Express Rider.")

ALL OFFSTAGE CAST: *(SING, O.S.)*
Pony Express rider! Pounding down the trail!
Pony Express rider! Bringing in the mail!

(LIGHTS UP LEFT on Bill and Pat at down left, shaking hands as if meeting after many months.)

PAT MCENEANEY: Bill Cody, you old picayune! I haven't seen you since the day we joined up fifteen months ago! But I've been reading about you from Salt Lake to Sacramento.

BILL CODY: I see you haven't lost your hair.

PAT MCENEANEY: *(rubs hip)* No, but I've gained a few saddle sores. Did you hear about the telegraph? They say it will reach across the whole country next month.

BILL CODY: I guess that spells the end of the Pony Express.

PAT MCENEANEY: Not at all. Who's going to carry the mail when the wire goes down? Believe me, Bill Cody—there's nothing this side of Pike's Peak can beat a fast horse and a smart rider.

(SOUND: loud hammer strike. Lights up center on Four Railroad Workers at center stage; two mime laying down a track that the other two mime pounding down with sledge-hammers.)

BILL: What in the world are those fellows doing?

PAT: Laying track for the Union Pacific Railroad. Poor lads…they'll never make it across the Rockies.

(LIGHTS OUT CENTER AND LEFT; LIGHTS UP RIGHT on Tim, Tina and Ms. Lopez at down right.)

MS. LOPEZ: Bill Cody was right about the end of the Pony Express. The first coast-to-coast telegraph connection was established October 24, 1861. A few Pony Express riders carried on for another month, and then the company disbanded. In another ten years, the transcontinental railroad would replace even most stage coach routes.

TIM: Well, that was a big waste of time, wasn't it? I mean, the Pony Express didn't stay in business two full years.

MS. LOPEZ: Trying to do your best is never a waste. You learn more about yourself when you face new challenges…and being a Pony Express rider in those days was certainly a challenge for anyone.

TINA: What happened to Bill and Pat?

MS. LOPEZ: Patrick McEneaney joined the U.S. calvary and served with the Union Army during the Civil War. He was decorated for bravery in battle several times.

TINA: And Bill Cody?

MS. LOPEZ: He became known as "Buffalo Bill" and created the Buffalo Bill Wild West Show, the biggest entertainment spectacle ever seen. He brought the excitement and wonder of the American West to people around the world.

TIM: *(staring at computer)* Look! The modem is working again!

TINA: I'm going to scream!

TIM: Now we can send our e-mail to Thailand. At last!

TINA: Say, Tim, did you hear about the new voice-activated microchip that transfers a file from one drive to another—just by talking to it?

TIM: Yeh, it'll put this old klunker on the shelf.

MS. LOPEZ: I don't know about that. Believe me—there's nothing this side of Pike's Peak can beat a fast modem and a smart hacker.

(Tim and Tina look quizically at Ms. Lopez; all three laugh. LIGHTS OUT.)

* THE END *

Pony Express Rider

(words & music by L.E. McCullough)

With a mer- ry lit- tle jog and a mer- ry lit- tle song
Whoa- ha! Buck and Jer- ry! We're rid- ing straight a- cross the
Wes- tern plains Whoa- ha! Buck and Jer- ry!
Po- ny Ex- press ri- der! Poun- ding down the trail!
Po- ny Ex- press ri- der! Bring- ing in the mail!

THE RAINBOW CRADLE

The Navajo are the largest Native American tribe in the United States, with over 130,000 members living in Arizona and New Mexico. The Navajo are part of the Athapascan cultural group, which migrated to the Southwest in the mid-1300s from northwestern Canada. Their traditional home quarters is called a *hogan*—a dome-shaped structure of logs and stone. The grandmother is the most important person in the traditional Navajo family, and her children and grandchildren are members of her clan. Navajo artists learned weaving from their Pueblo neighbors and learned silversmithing from Spanish settlers and are also well known for their pottery-making. The Navajo have many rituals that use music and dance and sandpainting; these rituals are led by a *shaman*, a person who possesses knowledge of the songs and knows how they are used in each ceremony.

TIME: 1876

PLACE: Navajo Reservation, Window Rock, Arizona Territory

CAST: 15 actors, min. 4 boys, 5 girls

Narrator #1 (Anglo)	Narrator #2 (Native American)
Three Stars (brother)	Bird-Comes-Back (sister)
Biwos (father)	Yellow Calf (mother)
Grandmother	First-Man
First-Woman	Sees-the-Wind (shaman)
Grey Flint (boy)	Feather Tree (girl)
Deer	Hunter
Blackbird	

RUNNING TIME: 15 minutes

STAGE SET: a scrim depicting a Navajo hogan and desert scene, a loom, a large boulder (mountain), a small rock

PROPS: wool, dirt, white-shell beads, white sheet, rainbow ribbon, 3 rattles, hunting bow, buckskin, sandpainting materials (sand, dirt, clay, 2 sticks)

EFFECTS: Visual—lightning flashes; Sound—thunder claps, wind noises

MUSIC: *The Rainbow Cradle, The Hunting Song*

COSTUMES: Narrator #1 dresses as an 1870s Anglo settler, Narrator #2 as an 1870s Native American; Navajo characters dress in 1870s Navajo attire—long, colorful calico skirts and velveteen blouses for women, dark breeches and vests for men, with moccasins, bright headbands, turquoise or silver jewelry for women and men; Deer can wear brown cape with antlers; Blackbird can be dressed in black with wings

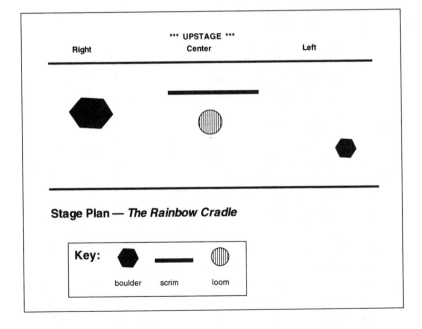

Stage Plan — *The Rainbow Cradle*

Key: boulder   scrim   loom

(LIGHTS UP RIGHT AND LEFT. Narrator #1 stands at down right; Narrator #2 stands at down left.)

NARRATOR #1: For many Americans, the year 1876 was a busy and exciting year. The Declaration of Independence had created the United States of America exactly one hundred years before, and folks back East were preparing for a great Centennial Celebration that would include parades and speeches and a big world's fair in Philadelphia, Pennsylvania.

NARRATOR #2: But in the West, the descendants of the very first Americans did not join in this celebration. Many Native American tribes were trying to protect their ancestral lands from encroaching settlers and were fighting the United States army. Other tribes, like the Navajo in the desert regions of the Southwest, had laid down their weapons. After surrendering to troops led by Colonel Kit Carson in 1868, they had agreed to live on reservations under the control of the Bureau of Indian Affairs, part of the United States government in Washington, D.C.

(LIGHTS DOWN RIGHT AND LEFT; LIGHTS UP CENTER where two women—Grandmother and Yellow Calf—sit carding wool for the loom.)

YELLOW CALF: *(calls out toward offstage left)* Three Stars! Bird-Comes-Back! Come here and help your grandmother and me with this wool! *(to Grandmother)* Sometimes I think my children have been swallowed by the Mountain Gods!

GRANDMOTHER: You must be more patient, Yellow Calf. When you were young and there was work to be done, you, too, were light-footed like the wind.

(Three Stars and Bird-Comes-Back skip in from left and cross to center, where they sit before Grandmother and Yellow Calf.)

THREE STARS: Mother, Grandmother! When will father be home? He promised he would take me hunting.

YELLOW CALF: Now, Three Stars, be careful how you talk. Your father, Biwos, was a great war chief when we fought the Americans, but he does not alone command *this* family.

GRANDMOTHER: Before every warrior learns to hunt, he must learn to weave. That is the way of the world.

(Yellow Calf hands batches of wool to Three Stars and Bird-Comes-Back, who begin carding it.)

BIRD-COMES-BACK: Grandmother, will you tell us the story of how the world began?

GRANDMOTHER: Yes, Bird-Comes-Back. It is a wonderful story. There are four worlds in our universe, one above another—the underworld, the middle world, our world on this earth, and the sky world above us. For many years The People did not live on the earth but lived in the underworld in the dark. One day, there arose a great flood, and The People were washed up through the middle world up onto the earth.

(LIGHTS FLASH AND FADE UP RIGHT on a boulder mid-right; SOUND CUE: THUNDER CLAPS, WIND NOISE. First-Man and First-Woman enter from right, cross to boulder.)

YELLOW CALF: First-Man and First-Woman were the first of The People to arrive. The earth was bare; there was nothing on it. So, First-Man and First-Woman began to make the world. They brought with them dirt from the underworld and made the sacred mountains of Navajo land.

(First-Man and First-Woman sprinkle dirt on boulder.)

GRANDMOTHER: Then they adorned the mountains with white shell and tied them to the earth with a bolt of lightning.

(First-Man and First-Woman place white-shell beads on boulder; LIGHTS FLASH; SOUND: thunder claps.)

YELLOW CALF: Then they covered the mountains with a sheet of daylight.

(First-Man and First-Woman cover boulder with sheet.)

GRANDMOTHER: First-Man and First-Woman continued to decorate the earth with clouds and sunbeams and turquoise.

YELLOW CALF: They brought up all the animals and trees and other People from the underworld.

GRANDMOTHER: Finally, they tied everything in the world together with a big rainbow.

(First-Man and First-Woman tie a large rainbow-colored ribbon around boulder, then exit right as LIGHTS FADE OUT RIGHT.)

BIRD-COMES-BACK: I saw a rainbow yesterday.

THREE STARS: What does it mean, Grandmother?

GRANDMOTHER: When you see a rainbow in the sky, it means a person's spirit is making a journey to the holy place beyond the sacred mountains. The spirit travels upon the rainbow, moving from mountain to mountain.

YELLOW CALF: And this is the song of the rainbow a mother sings to her children. The cradle is our world on earth, and the rainbow is our path to the world in the sky.

(Music: The Rainbow Cradle.)

YELLOW CALF: *(SINGS)*
    Hush, my little white shell
    In your rainbow cradle
    Do not cry, my white shell
    Do not cry, my white shell
ALL: *(SING)*
    Go to sleep my white shell
    Go to sleep my white shell
GRANDMOTHER: *(SINGS)*
    Rainbows lie beneath you
    Silver clouds around you
    Hush, my little white shell
    Do not cry, my white shell
ALL: *(SING)*
    Go to sleep my white shell
    Go to sleep my white shell
    Go to sleep my white shell

(LIGHTS UP LEFT on Biwos entering from left; Three Stars and Bird-Comes-Back run to him.)

THREE STARS & BIRD-COMES-BACK: Father! Father! Sing us a war song! Sing us a song of war!

BIWOS: Children, you must help your mother and grandmother with their work. Songs are not playthings or games. Songs are instruments of peace and blessing. They are the prayers of our people and protect us against evil. *(sits on rock at down left)* I will share a very powerful song with you.

(Three Stars and Bird-Comes-Back sit at his feet.)

BIWOS: In the old days, before the Navajo became shepherds and tillers of soil, we got all our food by hunting. The night before a hunt, Sees-the-Wind—our shaman—would lead us in making the hunting song.

(Sees-the-Wind enters from right shaking a rattle and humming the air to "The Hunting Song"; Grey Flint and Feather Tree follow him, each carrying materials for sandpainting as they cross to down center.)

SEES-THE-WIND: I am Sees-the-Wind, shaman to the Divine Ones...shaman to Blue Thunder and Black Thunder...shaman to Johano-ai, the Sun, and his Mother, She-Who-Changes, the Mother of all living things. *(beckons to Grey Flint and Feather Tree who place sandpainting materials on ground at down center)* Hear our song to the deer, O Divine Ones!

(Grey Flint and Feather Tree begin making sandpainting on buckskin as See-the-Wind hums and shakes rattle and dances around sandpainting.)

THREE STARS: What are Grey Flint and Feather Tree doing, father?

BIWOS: They are making a painting in the sand. Every song has its own painting.

BIRD-COMES-BACK: What is the painting about?

BIWOS: The painting tells the story of the song. It is made for the gods to whom the song is sung.

THREE STARS: Grey Flint is spreading out bee pollen and cornmeal.

BIRD-COMES-BACK: Yes, and clay and sand and charcoal.

BIWOS: This is how colors are made for the sandpainting. See how Feather Tree crushes rocks of different colors into fine powders? By mixing these with sand or dirt, she can make many kinds of paint.

(Sees-the-Wind stops dancing and kneels next to sandpainting, addressing it.)

SEES-THE-WIND
    May this offering be made to you,
    Mother Earth, Father Sky
    Meeting, joining one another
    Helpmates ever, they

(Sees-the-Wind stands, begins shaking rattle and singing "The Hunting Song"; Grey Flint and Feather Tree also shake rattles.)

SEES-THE-WIND: *(SINGS)*
    Comes the deer to my singing
    Comes the deer to my song
    Comes the deer to my singing
    Hi-ne-ye-yan-ga

(Deer enters from right, cautiously, sniffing the air.)

SEES-THE-WIND: *(SINGS)*
    He, the blackbird, he am I
    Bird beloved of the wild deer
    Comes the deer to my singing
    Hi-ne-ye-yan-ga

(Blackbird enters from left, crosses to deer at down right, dances before Deer and begins hypnotizing it.)

SEES-THE-WIND, GREY FLINT & FEATHER TREE: *(SING)*
    Through the blossoms, through the flowers
    Coming, coming now
    Comes the deer to my singing
ALL EXCEPT DEER & BLACKBIRD: *(SING)*
    Hi-ne-ye-yan-ga

(Hunter emerges from behind large boulder with bow; Deer turns and follows Hunter as Hunter walks in circle to where Hunter is at down right and Deer is at down left.)

SEES-THE-WIND, GREY FLINT & FEATHER TREE: *(SING)*
    Through the pollen, through the dew-drops
    Coming, coming now
    Comes the deer to my singing
ALL EXCEPT DEER, BLACKBIRD & HUNTER: *(SING)*
    Hi-ne-ye-yan-ga
    Hi-ne-ye-yan-ga
    Hi-ne-ye-yan-ga

(Hunter releases bow; Deer is struck and falls dead; music stops. Hunter and Blackbird stand over Deer; Sees-the-Wind, Grey Flint and Feather Tree shake rattles, and Hunter and Blackbird haul Deer offstage left; Sees-the-Wind, Grey Flint and Feather Tree exit behind Hunter, Blackbird and Deer.)

BIWOS: As he sang the song, Hunter changed into Blackbird, which is the favorite bird of Deer. Blackbird drew Deer closer and closer to Hunter, because Deer liked Hunter's song.
THREE STARS: I hope I can be a great hunter someday.
BIRD-COMES-BACK: Me, too, father.
BIWOS: You will both. But remember this: a good hunter needs more than a strong bow…
THREE STARS: A good hunter needs a strong heart…
BIRD-COMES-BACK: And a very strong song.

(LIGHTS OUT.)
* THE END *

The Rainbow Cradle

(traditional, arranged by L.E. McCullough)

Hush, my lit- tle white shell in your rain- bow cra- dle; Do not cry, my white shell, do not cry, my white shell; Go to sleep my white shell, go to sleep my white shell

The Hunting Song

(traditional, arranged by L.E. McCullough)

Comes the deer to my sing- ing Comes the deer to my song Comes the deer to my sing- ing Hi- ne- ye- yan- ga

ZEBRA DUN

Zebra Dun is a cowboy song from the late 1800s also known as *The Educated Feller*. Quite a lot of cowboy life on the trail and in the bunkhouse involved sitting around, and cowboys whiled away the idle hours composing poems and songs. *Zebra Dun* relates the story of a talkative, somewhat obnoxious stranger the cowboys suspect is a "greenhorn"—a person who pretends to know about cowboying but doesn't really know much at all. When the stranger asks to borrow a horse, the cowboys give him a mount that is still wild, expecting him to be unable to ride the animal. The stranger, however, quickly tames the horse, and the last laugh is on the cowboys. A "zebra dun" is a cowboy term for a brown horse with stripes usually along its back and shoulders and sometimes on its legs.

TIME: The 1870s or thereabouts

PLACE: Somewhere along the Old Chisholm Trail

CAST: 8 actors, min. 3 boys

Cookie	5 Cowboys
The Stranger	The Boss

RUNNING TIME: 15 minutes

STAGE SET: A two-foot length of corral fence at mid-right, a log or stump at mid-center

PROPS: bean pot, large cooking spoon, beans, plate, small eating spoon, lariat, stick horse

MUSIC: *Zebra Dun*. The verses are sung to two melodies, designated by Verse A or Verse B, along with the Final Tag melody. Several recordings of *Zebra Dun* exist on anthologies of cowboy and Western music; check them out to make your style and delivery more authentic.

COSTUMES: Cowboys, Cookie and The Boss wear standard 1870s cowboy clothes—Cookie wears an apron; The Stranger wears a citified, store-bought suit and hat; the stick horse can be a simple broom stick with a horse head or mask

PERFORMANCE NOTE: Except where indicated, characters should speak and sing their lines to the audience; a good deal of mime can be used throughout to support the narrative.

(LIGHTS UP FULL on a cattle drive camp site. Five Cowboys lounge in a semi-circle at center stage, from left to right: Cowboy #1 stands, Cowboy #2 sits on ground wth legs crossed, Cowboy #3 sits on log, Cowboy #4 lies on the ground, head propped on an elbow, Cowboy #5 squats on legs. Cookie is at down right, stirring beans in a pot; he pauses and addresses the audience.)

COOKIE: Folks think cowboys are a serious bunch. That's because on the cattle drive, cowboys are kept awful busy ropin' steers and shootin' varmints and fightin' off stampedes and rustlers and rattlesnakes and such. But real cowboys *do* have a sense of humor. They love a good joke as much as the next person. And they know how to take a joke on themselves. Like the day The Stranger walked into camp...

(The Stranger enters from left and greets Cowboys; Cowboy #5 shakes The Stranger's hand and introduces him to other Cowboys. MUSIC: Zebra Dun.)

COOKIE: *(SINGS) [Verse A]*
We were camped out on the plains at the head of Cimarron,
When along come a stranger, and he stopped to argue some.
He looked so very foolish, we begun to scout around,
And we think he is a greenhorn and just escaped from town.

(Cookie spoons out beans onto a plate, hands plate to Cowboy #2 who hands it to The Stranger; Cowboy #3 gets up from log and invites The Stranger to sit; The Stranger sits and begins discoursing with expansive gestures to Cowboys gathered around him.)

COWBOY #1: *(SINGS) [Verse A]*
We asked him if he'd had a bite, and he hadn't had a smear;
So we opened up the chuckbox and forked him out a share.
He took a cup of coffee, some biscuits and some beans
And then begun to talk about those foreign kings and queens.

COWBOY #2: *(SINGS)* *[Verse B]*

> And all about the Spanish War and fighting on the seas
> With pistols big as Texas steers and rifles big as trees,
> And all about John Paul Jones, that fighting son-of-a-drum;
> He said he was the rankest cuss that ever drawed a gun.

(Cowboys put hands over ears, turn away from The Stranger, do "gag" sign and other gestures of disbelief; Cowboy #1 nudges Cowboy #2 and whispers in his ear; Cowboy #2 nods "yes" and beckons to Cowboy #3 behind the back of The Stranger, who is unaware of his audience's reactions; Cowboy #2 whispers to Cowboy #3 who whispers to Cowboy #4 who whispers to Cowboy #5.)

COWBOY #3: *(SINGS)* *[Verse B]*

> Such an educated feller, his thoughts just ran in herds,
> And every living sentence had ten jaw-breaking words;
> But he just kept on talking—till it made us all darn sick,
> And we began to figure out just how to play a trick.

COWBOY #4: *(SINGS)* *[Verse A]*

> Well, he said he had just lost his job upon the Sante Fe,
> And he was going across the plains to strike the O.F.D.
> He didn't say how come it—some trouble with the boss—
> But he asked if he might borrow—

THE STRANGER: A nice fresh saddle horse?

(Cowboys and Cookie snicker; Cowboy #1 takes the lariat from his waist and "ropes" the stick horse leaning against the corral fence, tugging it to center stage with help of Cowboys #2, 3, 4 and 5.)

COWBOY #5: *(SINGS)* *[Verse B]*

> Now, this tickled all the boys to death; they laughed right up
>   their sleeves.
> "Oh, we'll give you a horse just as fresh as you please!"
> Shorty grabbed a lariat, and he roped old Zebra Dun,
> And then the boys all settled back and waited for the fun.

(Cowboys "pacify" the skittish horse and present it to The Stranger, releasing the rope and backing away quickly as The Stranger stands and regards the horse with curiosity.)

COOKIE: (SINGS) [Verse B]
Now Dunnie was an outlaw grown so awful wild,
That he could paw the moon, boys, and jump up for a mile.
But old Dun, he just stood right still, as if he did not know—
Until they got him saddled up and ready for the show.

(The Stranger saddles the horse, and the horse—in actuality
a dangerous, unbroken bronco—flies up and goes wild, dragging him around the stage as the Cowboys and Cookie laugh,
point, slap thighs and hoot.)

COWBOY #1: (SINGS) [Verse B]
When the stranger hit the saddle, old Dunnie quit the earth,
And he traveled right straight up for all that he was worth—
A-pitching and a-squealing and having wall-eyed fits,
His hind feet perpendicular, his front feet in the bits.

(Cowboys and Cookie look up toward sky and then down at
ground as if horse has indeed leapt high into the air and then
hurtled to earth; they stare as The Stranger stops at down
center and sits tall in the saddle.)

COWBOY #2: (SINGS) [Verse B]
You could see those snowy mountains under Dunnie every jump,
But the stranger, he was growed there just like the camel's hump.
He leaned back in the saddle, and he twirled his black mustache,
Just like some summer boarder a-waiting for his hash.

THE STRANGER: (to horse) Giddyap, Old Dunnie!

(The Stranger whirls horse around and lopes gently around
the stage, stopping at down center and dismounting, hand-
ing the horse to Cowboy #2; Cowboy #2 returns horse to fence
as The Stranger shakes hands with the other cowboys.)

COWBOY #3: *(SINGS)* *[Verse B]*
>   He punched him in the shoulder, and he spurred him when he
>   whirled
>   To show those earth-bound cowpokes he was the top wolf of
>   the world.
>   When the stranger had dismounted once more upon the
>   ground,
>   We knew he was the salty dog and not no boy from town.

(The Boss enters from left and approaches The Stranger.)

COWBOY #4: *(SINGS)* *[Verse B]*
>   Well, the boss he had been standing and a-watching of the show.
>   He walked up to the stranger and he said,

BOSS: *(SINGS)* *[Verse B, cont.]*
>   "You need not go.
>   If you can use a catch-rope like you rode old Zebra Dun,
>   Then you're the man I've been looking for since the Year of One!"

(Cowboy #1 hands lariat to The Stranger, who twirls it as if roping steers; Cowboys are impressed and nudge each other and nod.)

COWBOY #5: *(SINGS)* *[Verse B]*
>   Now, he sure could use a catch-rope, and he did not use it slow;
>   He sure could forefoot 'em ten times there in a row.
>   And when the herd stampeded, he was always on the spot
>   To set those critters milling like the boiling of a pot.

(Cowboys and Boss sit and lie down in semi-circle at mid-center behind The Stranger, who steps forward to down center, dangling his lariat.)

COOKIE: *(SINGS)* *[Final Tag]*
>   Now there's one thing, and it's a sure thing I've learned since I
>   was born—
THE STRANGER: *(SINGS)* *[Final Tag]*
>   Every educated feller ain't no darn plumb greenhorn!

(LIGHTS OUT.)   * THE END *

Zebra Dun

(traditional, arr. by L.E. McCullough)

∞ *Verse A* ∞

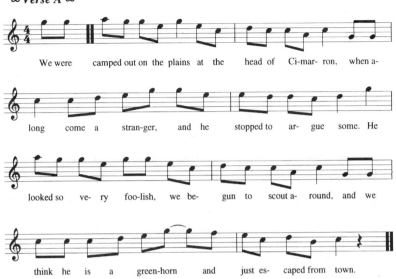

We were camped out on the plains at the head of Ci-mar-ron, when a-long come a stran-ger, and he stopped to ar-gue some. He looked so ve-ry foo-lish, we be-gun to scout a-round, and we think he is a green-horn and just es-caped from town.

Zebra Dun

∞ *Verse B* ∞

And all a-bout the Span-ish War and fight-ing on the seas with pis-tols big as Tex-as steers and ri-fles big as trees, And all a-bout — John Paul Jones, that fight-ing son-of-a-drum; He said he was the rank-est cuss that ev-er drawed a gun.

Zebra Dun

∞ *Final Tag* ∞

Well, there's one thing, and it's a sure thing I've

learned since I was born Eve- ry ed- u- ca- ted

fel- ler ain't no darn plumb green- horn!

A NOTE ON COSTUMES & SETS

If you are interested in creating really authentic costumes and material culture artifacts for your *Plays of the Wild West* productions, there are numerous books at your local library that tell how to do so. For individuals, you can consult biographies. Books on Annie Oakley and Buffalo Bill, for instance, offer detailed descriptions of what they wore along with photographs and portraits. Magazines such as *American Heritage*, *American History*, *Old West* and *True West* are also excellent sources for costume detail. Below are just a few books I discovered in the card catalogue at my local branch library:

- *Indian Clothing of the Great Lakes, 1740-1840*. Sheryl Hartman. Liberty, UT: Eagle's View Publishing. 391.0097

- *Traditional Dress: A Good Medicine Book*. Adolf Hungry Wolf. Summertown, TN: Book Publishing Co. 391.009701

- *Historic Dress of the Old West*. Ernest Lisle Reedstrom. New York, NY: Sterling Publishing. Also titled *Authentic Costume and Characters of the Wild West*. 391.0978

- *Calico Chronicle: Texas Women and Their Fashions, 1830-1910*. Betty J. Mills. Lubbock, TX: Texas Tech Press. 391.0976

- *Ceremonial Costumes of the Pueblo Indians*. Virginia More Roediger. Berkeley, CA: University of California Press. 391.09706

- *Mexican Indian Costumes*. Donald Bush Cordry. Austin, TX: University of Texas Press. 391.0972

- *Encyclopedia of American Indian Costumes*. Josephine Paterek. Denver, CO: ABC-CLIO. 391.09703

- *Cowboy Gear: A Photographic Portrayal of the Early Cowboys and Their Equipment*. Donald R. Stoecklein. Ketchum, ID: Dober Hill Press. 391.0978

- *100 Years of Western Wear*. Tyler Beard. Salt Lake City, UT: Gibbs-Smith Press. 391.0978

- *The Look of the Old West*. William Foster Harris. New York, NY: Viking Press. 917.8

- *Mexican Costume*. Carlos Merida. Chicago, IL: Pocahontas Press. 391.0972

- *$10 Horse, $40 Saddle: Cowboy Clothing, Arms, Tools and Horse Gear of the 1880s*. Don Rickey. Ft. Collins, CO: Old Army Press. 391.0978

- *Warbonnets*. Rod Peate. Denison, TX: Crazy Crow Trading Post. 391.09701

- **Anything** by author David Dary, whose comprehensive social histories of the American West include photographs, drawings and diagrams. Check out his *Seeking Pleasure in the Old West* (978), *The Buffalo Book* (559.7358), *Cowboy Culture* (978) and *Entrepreneurs of the Old West* (338.040978).

- *What People Wore: A Visual History of Dress from Ancient Times to 20th-Century America*. Douglas Gorsline. New York, NY: Dover Books. 391.09. This has a *huge* bibliography of other costume books.